GLOBAL CRISES, RANDOM OR PLANNED?

GEO-POLITICAL, ECONOMIC AND ISLAMIC PERSPECTIVES

ALHAMDULILLAH E RAB AL A'ALAMEEN (THANKS TO ALLAH THE ALMIGHTY), I HAVE PUT IN MY BEST AND SINCERE EFFORT TO GET TO THE TRUTH ON THIS SUBJECT.

IT IS AN HUMBLE EFFORT TO OPEN THE DOOR OF KNOWLEDGE FOR THOSE WHO HAVE THE QUEST FOR STRIVING FURTHER TOWARD CONNECTING THE DOTS AND SEEKING TRUTH!

AND I WILL ALWAYS SAY "ALLAH KNOWS BEST!"

I dedicate this book to all "Truth Seekers", who have the quest for seeking knowledge (Truth in every field of knowledge) and intend to follow and propagate the Truth!

CONTENTS

FOREWORD

Alhamdolillah (By the Grace of God The Al Mighty), I present my thoroughly researched understanding about the **Crises happening worldwide** in terms not only **What, but Why and Who are responsible behind the scenes**.

This Book will give the respected reader **insight with a broader horizon** about the agenda of the "**hidden hands**", who are responsible for **humanity's miseries, destitution, and ultimate enslavement!** It is high time that we must be aware of these "blood sucking monsters" and their "networks", so that the **humanity may wake up and stop acquiescing** to the "**Tiny Oppressive Group**" (**with borderless overt and covert connections**) ruling over mankind and **try to achieve REAL FREEDOM**!

I have tried to unfold the reasons that why the "**few psychopathic demonic people, on top of the pyramid**" are obsessed to attain "**full spectrum domination**" of mankind and the resources worldwide?

While discussing "Crises" in general, my **focus will be toward Middle Eastern Region**, which is in turmoil for **more than thirty years** and **still at the world's centre stage!** This will cover **Iraq, Libya, Palestine, Iran and Syria**. Several issues / crises related to these countries will also be covered here.

I have humbly attempted to present **current and future happenings,** based on **geo-political, economic, and Islamic Eschatological perspectives**, so that the reader may be able to have a comprehensive understanding on the issues.

Since, I anticipate **difficult times ahead** by viewing the bigger picture in greater depth, therefore **suggested various critical steps to be taken toward safeguarding not only oneself but families and friends worldwide!**

Happy reading!

SEEING THE BIGGER PICTURE

PUPPET MASTERS CONTROL THE SO-CALLED LEADERS APPEARING ON THE WORLD SCENE!

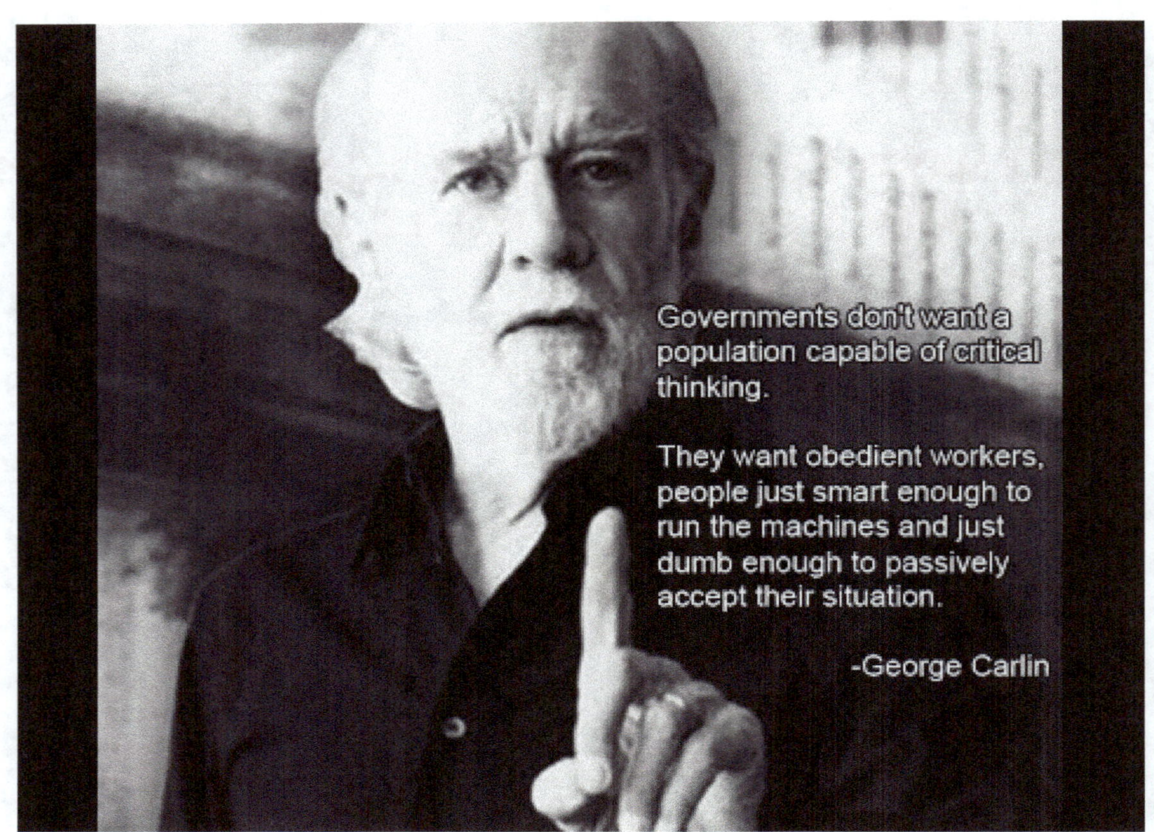

WORLD RULING "EVIL DEMONIC, PSYCHOPATHIC ELITE"

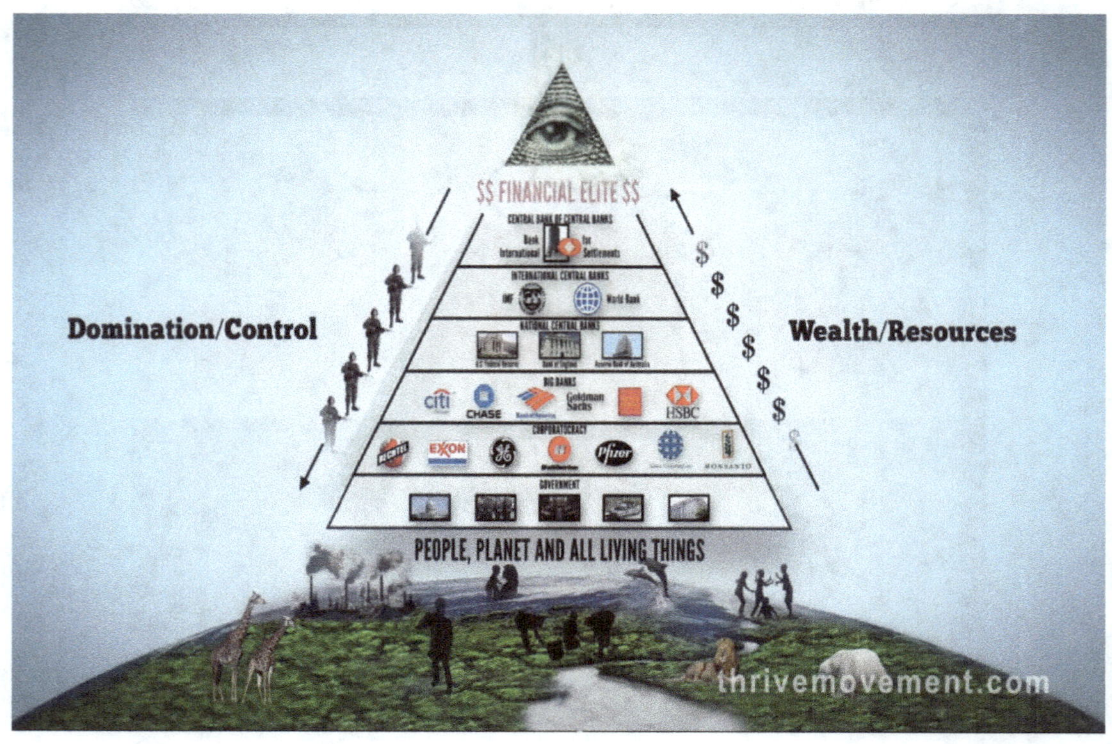

DECODING TERMS….

"Globalists", "They", "Elite", "Secret Cabal", "Shadow Government", "Secret Societies", "Hidden Hand"

Are These Synonyms?

Who Are These People??

Let's Dive In The Rabbit Hole and Explore!

WHO RULES THE WORLD?

ROTHSCHILD FAMILY - AXIS OF EVIL!

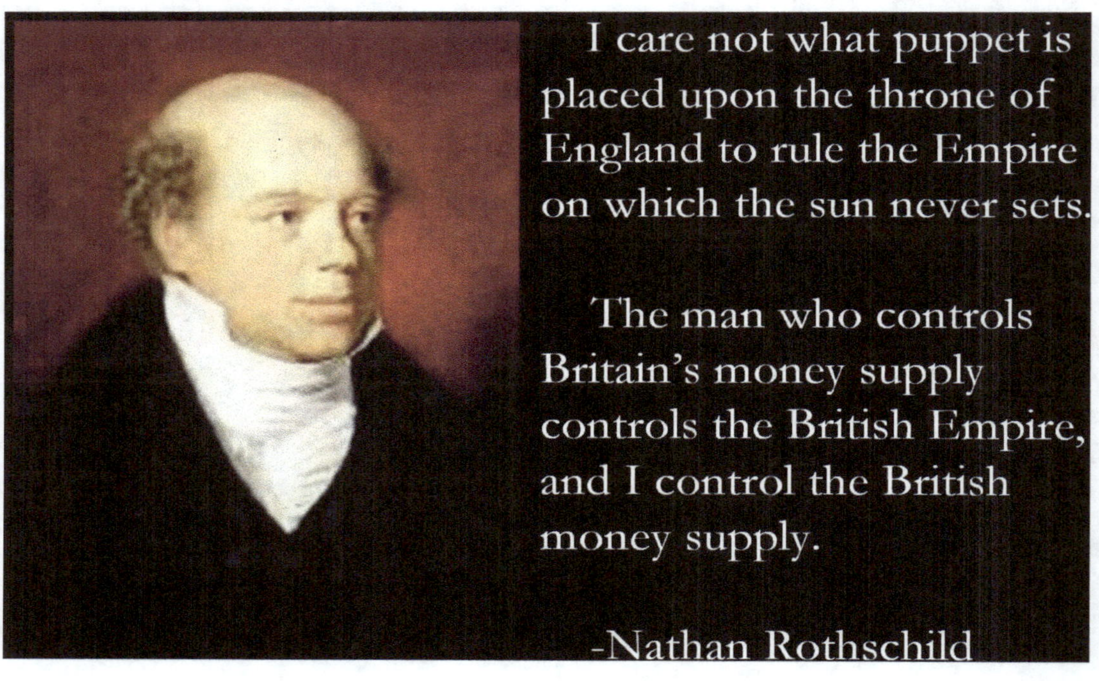

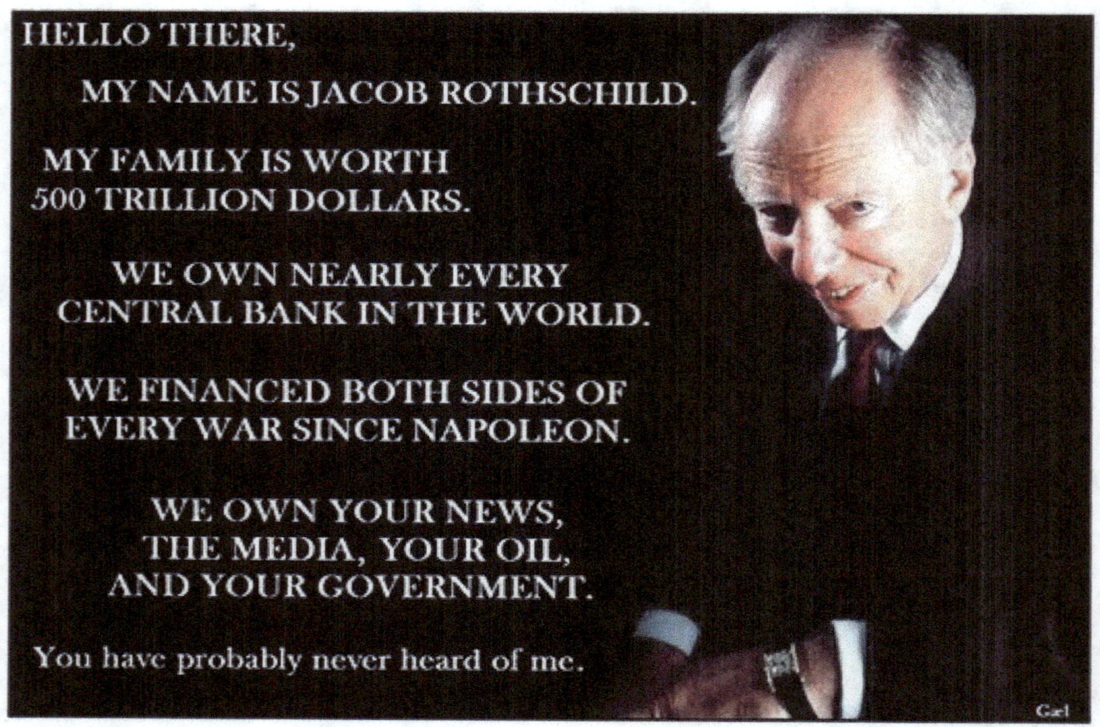

ROTHSCHILD'S FAMILY MASSIVE WEALTH POWER COMES FROM THE BANKING SYSTEM (AXIS OF EVIL)!

They own and control 165 central banks / monetary agencies of the world, Libya is the recent conquest, while Somalia & Syria is on its way!

Two of the world's largest banks: World bank is jointly owned by the top banking families; IMF is privately owned by the Rothschild alone!

- These **Two Mega Banks** offer loans (fictitious fraud, paper currency) to "developing countries" (forcibly or otherwise) and use their almost impossible-to-pay-back interests to get their hands on the real wealth: **Land / Strategic Assets** and **Natural Resources & Precious Metals**!

- Rothschild are behind all wars since Napoleon, as they found it to be profitable to finance both sides of the war!

In 1849, Guttle Schnapper, the wife of Mayer Amschel (Rothschild) stated: **"If my sons did not want wars, there would be none."**

So, the world is **still and will remain at war** because it is very, very profitable to the Rothschilds and their parasite bankster bloodlines. And for as long as we will continue to use "fraudulent fiat / fake paper currency", the world will never be at peace!!

In 1835, US **President Andrew Jackson** declared his disregard for the international bankers: **"You are a den of vipers. I intend to rout you out, and by the Eternal God, I will rout you out.** If the people only understood the rank injustice of our money and banking system, there would be a revolution before morning."

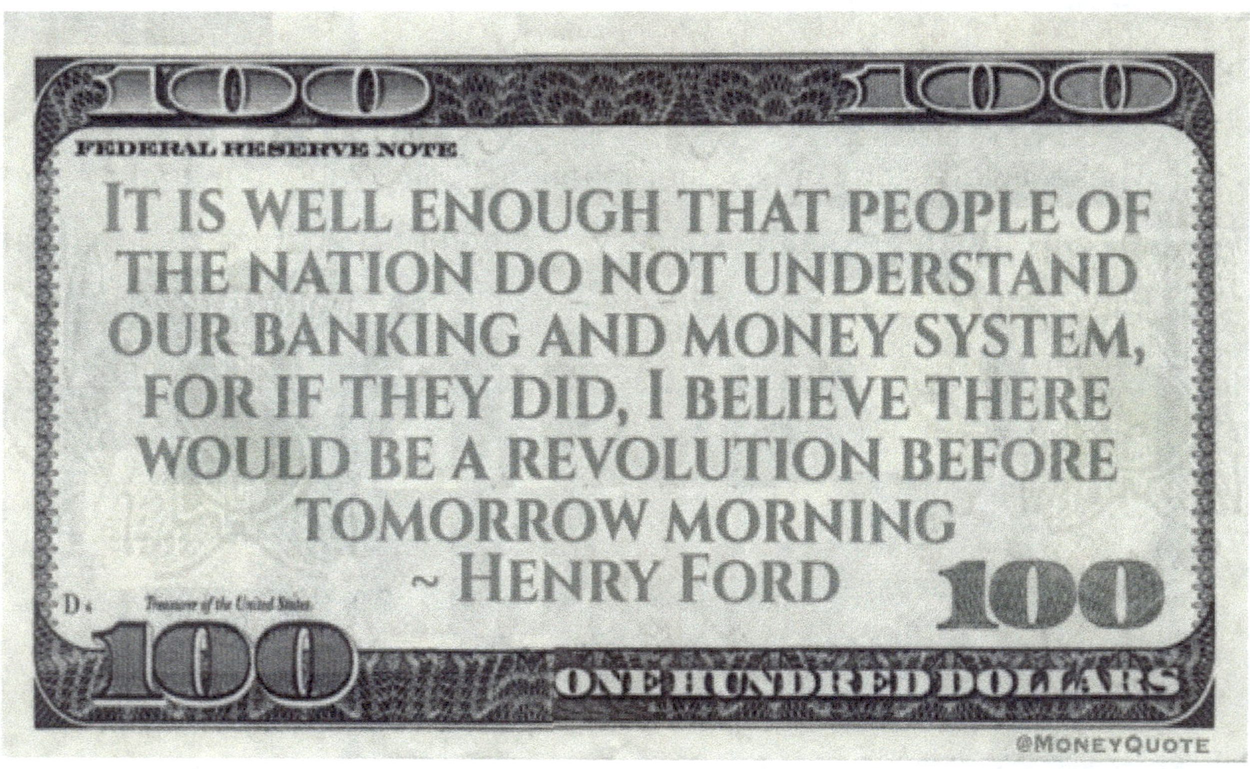

OWNERS OF SECRET SOCIETIES - "COUNCIL OF THE 13 FAMILIES"

Rothschild (Bauer or Bower) – Controls Global Banking System etc. (Assets worth Trillions!!)

Bruce

Cavendish (Kennedy)

De Medici

Hanover

Hapsburg

Krupp

Plantagenet

Rockefeller - Controls US Military Industrial Complex, Major Oil Companies etc. (Assets worth over $340 Billion!)

Romanov

Sinclair (St. Clair)

Warburg (del Banco)

Windsor (Saxe-Coburg-Gothe)

"Some even believe we are part of a secret cabal working against the best interests of the United States, characterizing my family and me as 'internationalists' and of conspiring with others around the world to build a more integrated global political and economic structure – one world, if you will. If that's the charge, I stand guilty, and I am proud of it."
-- David Rockefeller, from his own book, "Memoirs".

"This present window of opportunity, during which a truly peaceful and interdependent world order might be built, will not be open for too long. We are on the verge of a global transformation. All we need is the right major crisis and the nations will accept the NEW WORLD ORDER"
- David Rockefeller, 1994

TRINITY OF WORLD POWER

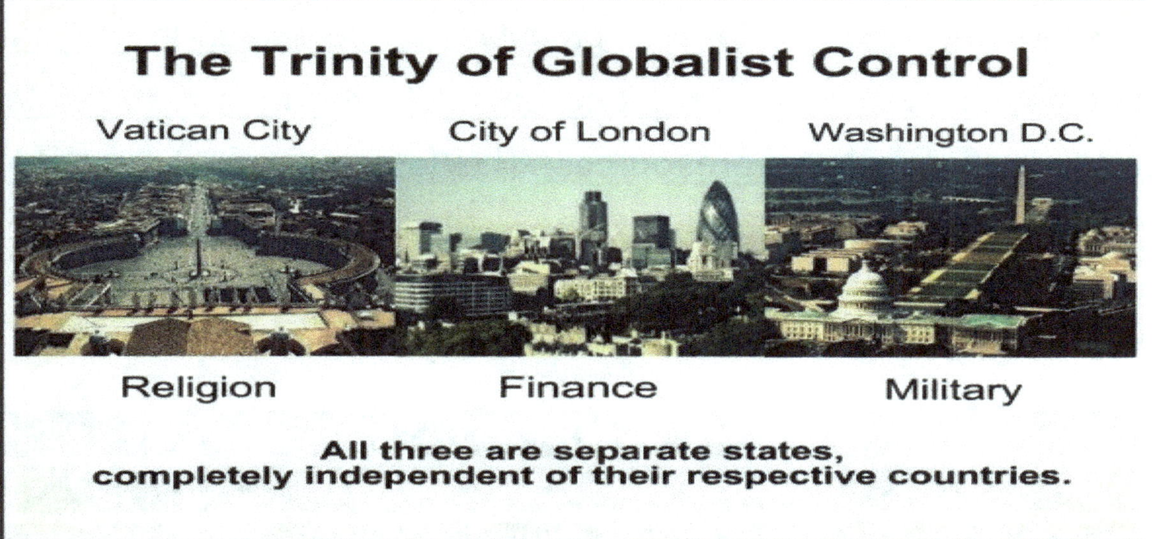

CENTRES / INSTITUTIONS AIMED AT IMPLEMENTING "NEW WORLD ORDER" FOR ENSLAVING HUMANITY!

- **The City of London** (Finance, controlled by the Rothschilds) – 644 Acre Independent State **NOT part of the UK.**

- **The US Federal Reserve** (Finance – 100% Private Bank (Printing Press of USD), owned by the Rothschilds + 11 Private Banks) - **NOT part of the USA.**

- **The Vatican City** (Indoctrination, Deception and Scare Tactics) – Independent State **NOT part of Italy.**

- **Washington D.C.** (Military, Mind Programming, Brainwashing, Humanization, Depopulation, Evil Social Experimentation / Fear Mongering etc.) **- NOT part of the USA.**

EXPOSING THE PREDATORY RULING ELITE NETWORK

There are very few people, who probably <u>can be seated in a room</u>, but these **psychopathic, demonic and satanists group lust to "Rule the World" both people and resources!** They operate through a **worldwide complex network**, which has no borders. Please see a glimpse below:

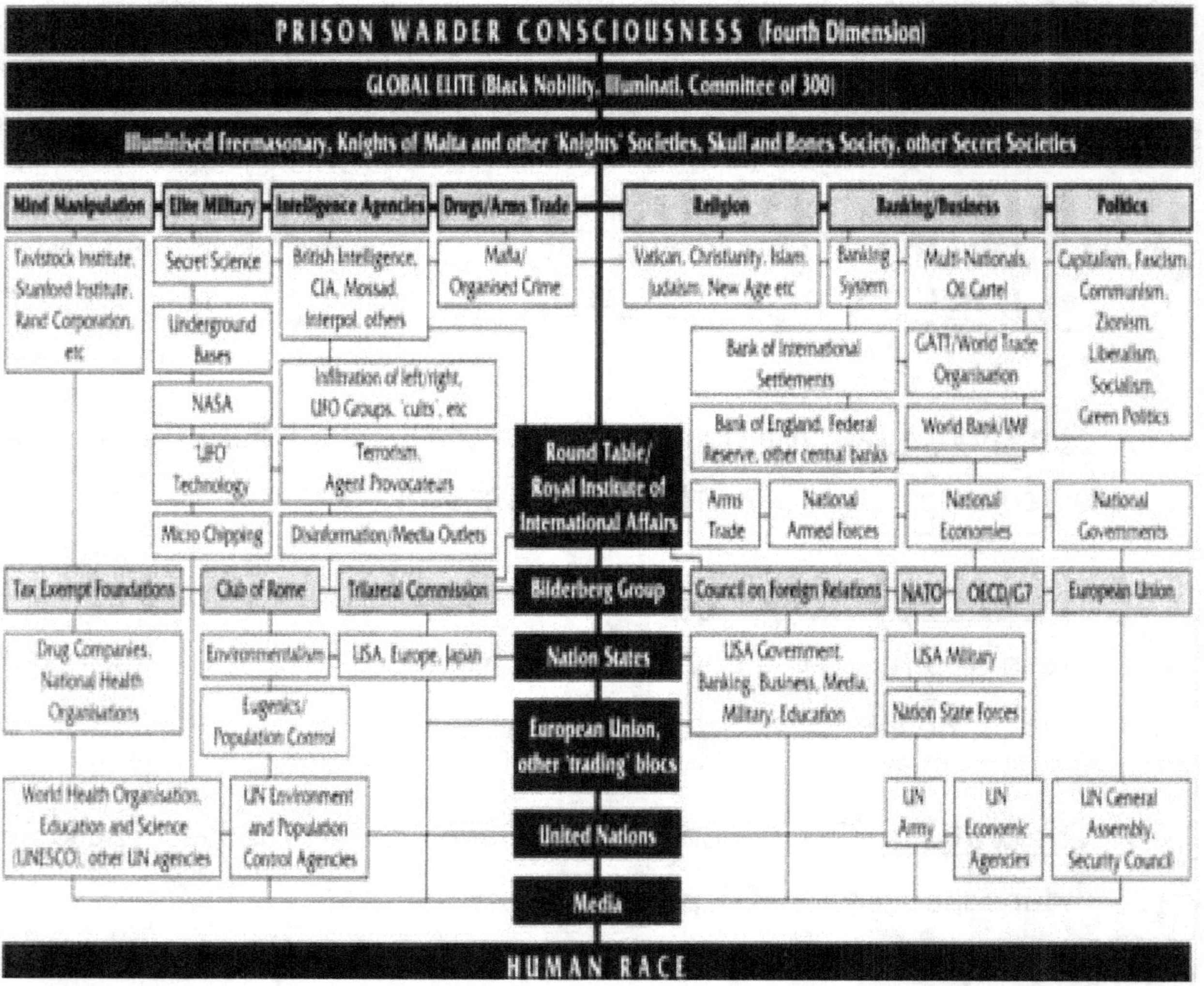

For your kind reference, please read an article:
http://www.newdawnmagazine.com/articles/the-elite-the-great-game-world-war-iii
By: Prof Dr. Mujahid Kamran, VC Punjab University

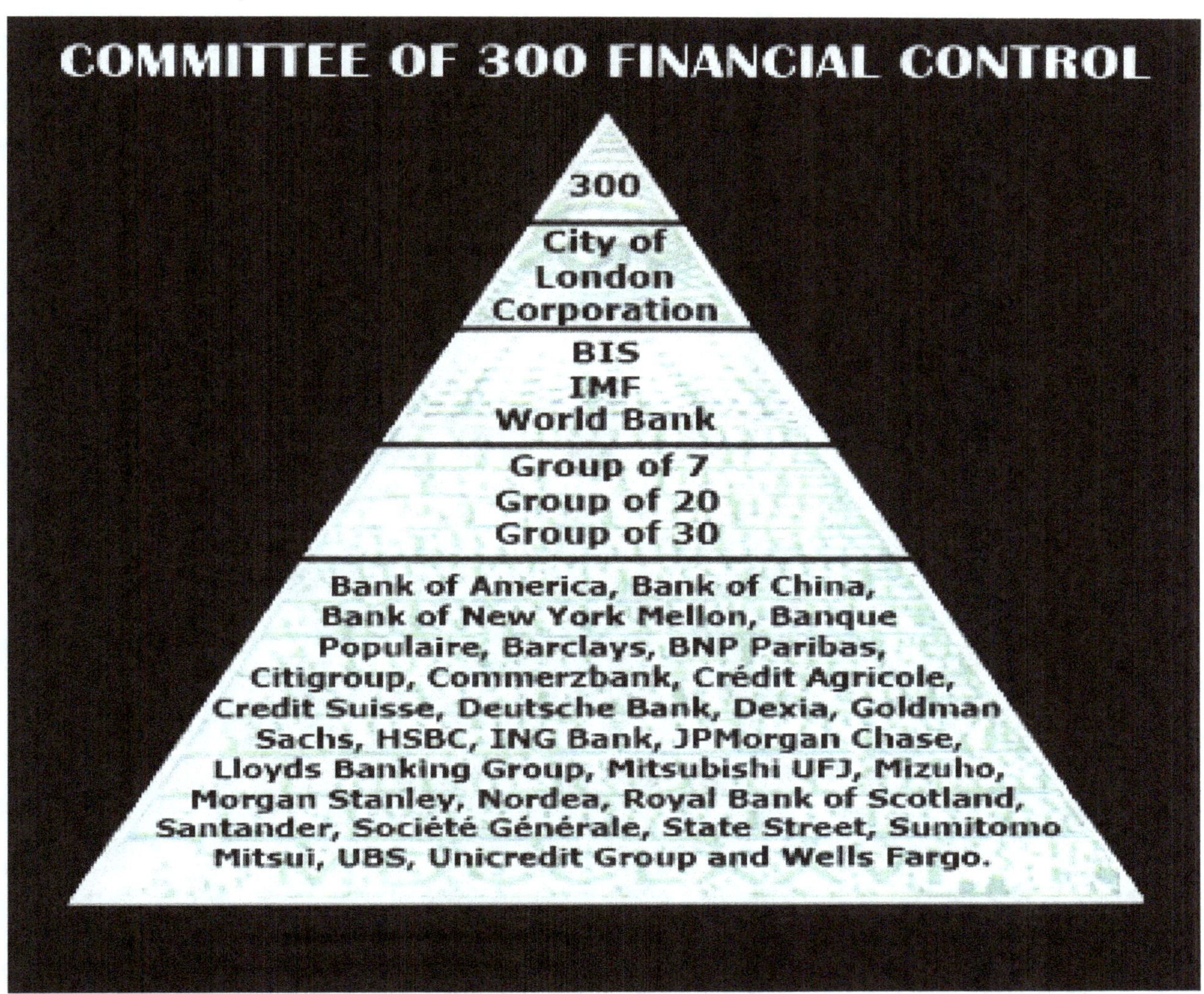

Dr. John Coleman (Ex-MI5 Agent) Disclosure of the "Committee of 300" - [Predatory Global Ruling Elite]

ROTHSCHILD'S – ZIONIST CONNECTION!

LEADER OF "GLOBALIST SECRET SOCIETIES" FOR ACHIEVING WORLDWIDE POLITICAL AND ECONOMIC CONTROL!

ESTABLISHMENT OF ZIONIST MOVEMENT – 1897 CE

These Jewish bankers (controlled by the **Rothschild Family**) at this moment of time gained control of almost all the known resources and economies in Europe, America, South Asia, Far East and South Africa, gathered in Basel – Switzerland, bold enough to declare the "Protocols of the Elders of Zion". Some of the key postulates summarised as follows:

Global Agenda:

- ❖ Establishment of secularism /godlessness across the world

- ❖ Controlling of entire world economy through **interest-based**

  banking system

- ❖ Propagating **vulgarity and pornography** by all possible means

(to

  destroy the religious way of life and decent social systems
  across all civilizations)

Regional Agenda:

- ❖ Launching of **Armageddon** (Big wars between good and evil
forces

  before the end time), which is full scale **WWIII** to reshape the

Middle

  East map for **the creation of Greater Israel**

- ❖ Destroying of Al Aqsa and Dome of Rock Mosques

- ❖ Construction of 3rd Temple in Bait Al Maqdas (Jerusalem)

- ❖ Placement of the Throne of David (currently in Westminster Abbey

  Church) in the **3rd Temple**

- ❖ Establishment of Israel as the Ruling State of the World to pave the

way of their so-called Messiah (**False Messiah/ Anti-Christ / Dajjal**)
to the rule the world from there, which according to them will be the
Eternal Rule.

BALFOUR DECLARATION BY BRITISH EMPIRE – 1917 CE

The Balfour Declaration was a November 2, 1917, letter from British
Foreign Secretary Arthur James Balfour to Lord Rothschild (Chairman
Zionist Movement) that made public the British support of a Jewish
homeland in Palestine. The Balfour Declaration led the League of
Nations to entrust the United Kingdom with the Palestine Mandate in
1922.

The excerpt of the original declaration is as follows:

The Balfour Declaration (it its entirety)

Foreign Office
November 2nd, 1917

Dear Lord Rothschild,

*I have much pleasure in conveying to you, on behalf of His
Majesty's Government, the following declaration of sympathy
with Jewish Zionist aspirations which has been submitted to,
and approved by, the Cabinet.*

"His Majesty's Government view with favour the establishment in Palestine of a national home for the Jewish people and will use their best endeavours to facilitate the achievement of this object, it being clearly understood that nothing shall be done which may prejudice the civil and religious rights of existing non-Jewish communities in Palestine, or the rights and political status enjoyed by Jews in any other country."

I should be grateful if you would bring this declaration to the knowledge of the Zionist Federation.

Yours sincerely,
Arthur James Balfour

CONTROLLING BIG POWERS – A GLIMPSE!

(ROTHSCHILD ZIONSTS THROUGH THEIR AGENTS CONTROLLING THE BIG POWERS!)

RAHM EMANUEL – WHITE HOUSE CHIEF OF STAFF

GEORGE SOROS – MAIN FUNDER OF OBAMA AND COLOUR REVOLUTIONS ACROSS EAST EUROPE, MIGRANT MOVEMENT (SYRIAN CRISIS), UKRAINE!

HENRY KISSINGER – BIG TIME WAR MONGER CRIMINAL, RESPONSIBLE FOR INNUMERABLE KILLINGS AND GURU FOR US POLICY MAKERS SINCE 1971...

WHO CONTROLS BRITISH POLITICS?

MEDIA PROPAGANDA VS TRUTH

96% of world mainstream media is controlled by Six Jewish companies

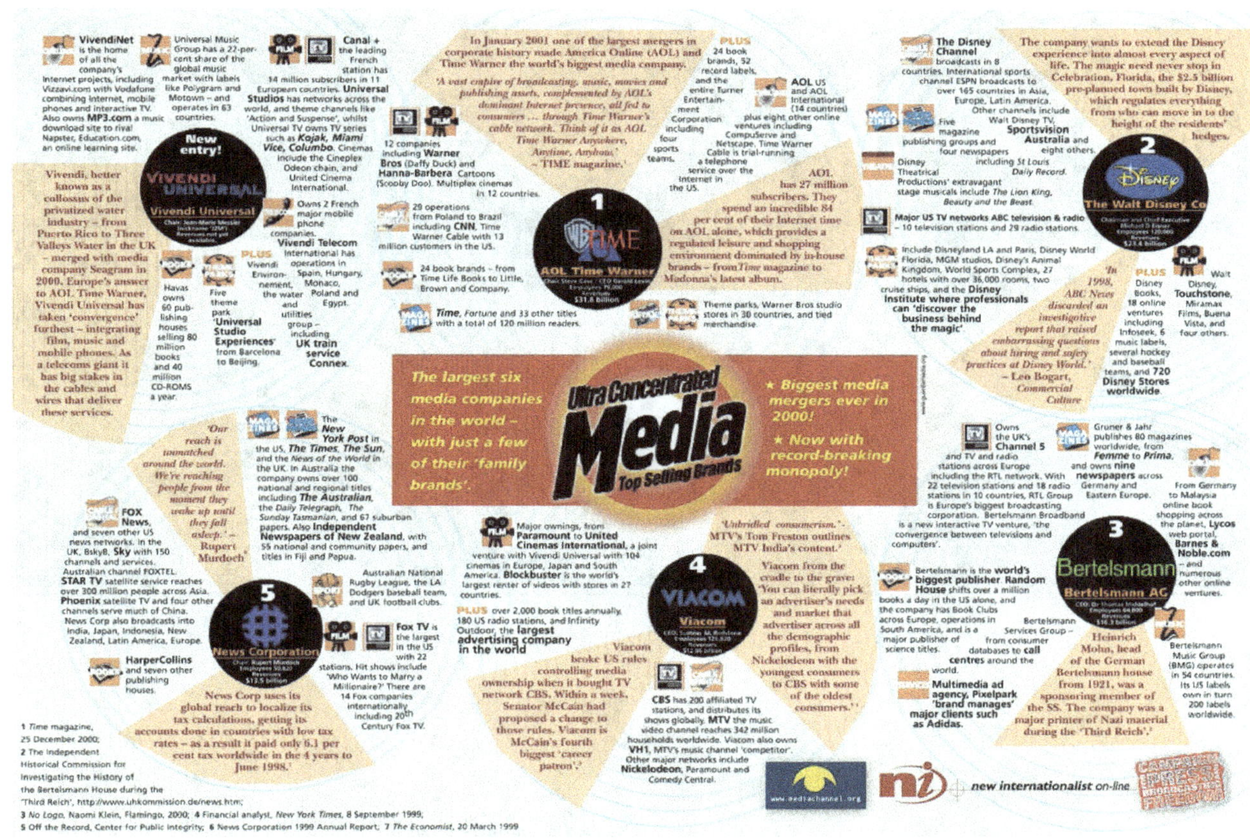

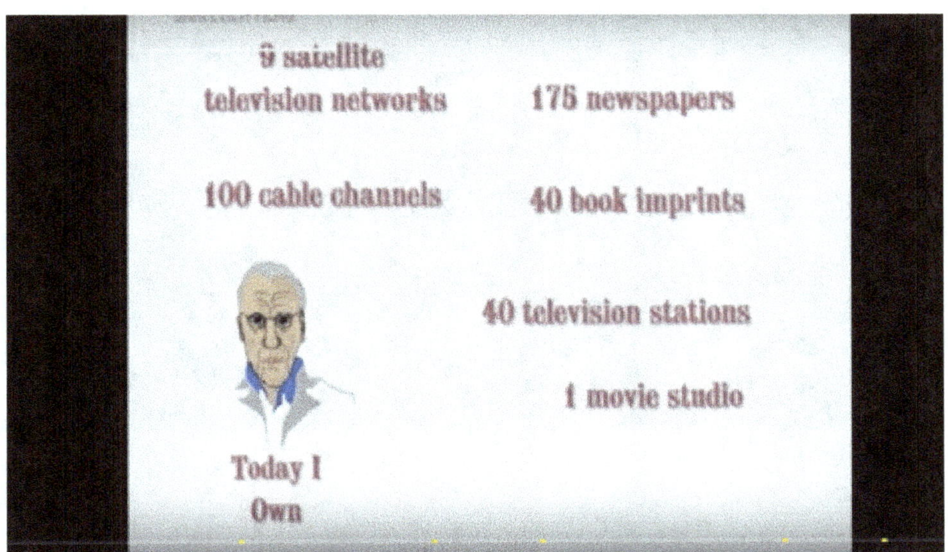

I AM RUPERT MURDOCH!!

THE PRINT AND ELCTRONIC MEDIA HAS BEEN CONTROLLED SINCE TIME AND MEMORIAL!

There is no such thing in America as an independent press.... There is not one of you who dares to write your honest opinions, and if you did, you know beforehand that it would never appear in print. I am paid $150 a week for keeping my honest opinions out of the paper I am connected with.

(John Swinton)

The duty of journalists is to tell the truth. Journalism means you go back to the actual facts, you look at the documents, you discover what the record is, and you report it that way.

—NOAM CHOMSKY, professor and author

BUT SPEAKING, WRITING AND STANDING FOR TRUTH IS A GREAT CHALLENGE!

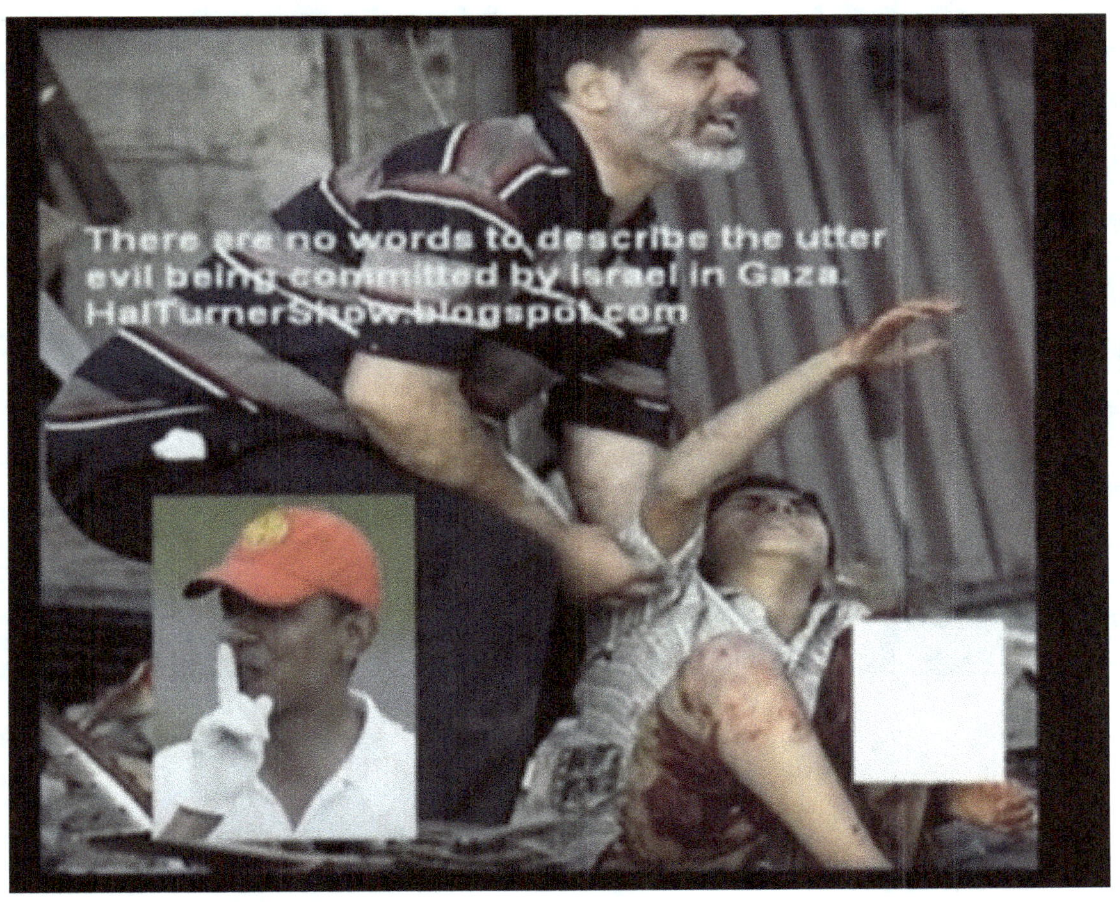

A JEW JAILED FOR 18 YEARS FOR TELLING THE TRUTH!!

THEY DON'T SPARE ANY VOICE OF TRUTH OR AGAINST ZIONIST OPPRESSION! AN AMERICAN JOURNALIST, RACHEL CONFRONTING AN ISRAELI SOLDIER AGAINST THE DEMOLITION OF PALESTINIANS HOLMES WAS KILLED!!

"THERE ARE LIES, SOME ARE OTHER BIGGER LIES AND SOMETHING BIGGEST IS 9/11"

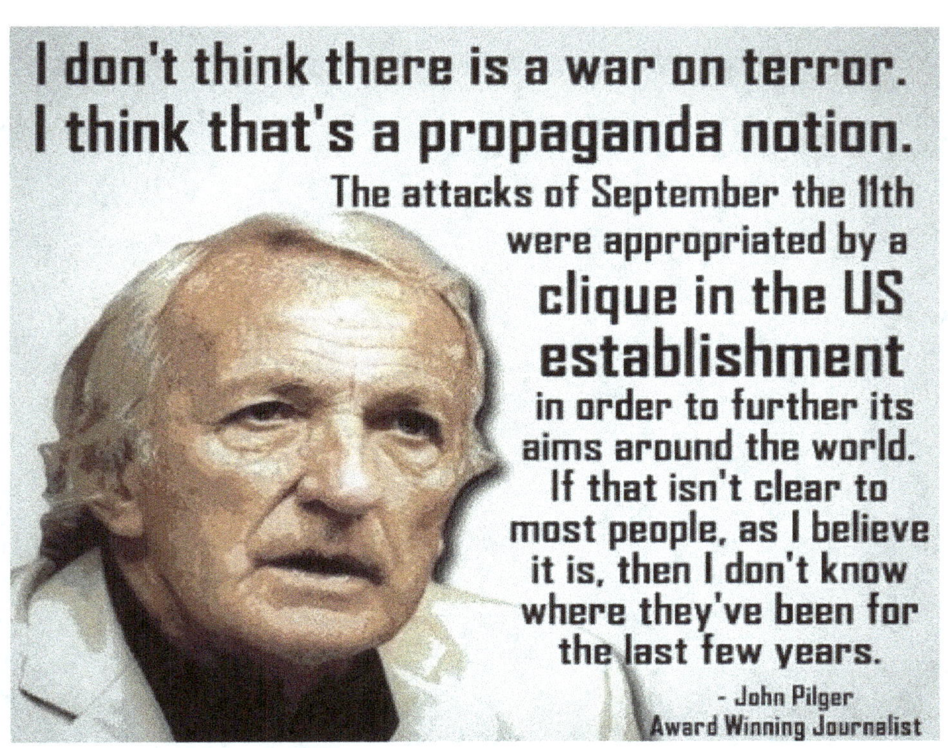

I don't think there is a war on terror. I think that's a propaganda notion. The attacks of September the 11th were appropriated by a clique in the US establishment in order to further its aims around the world. If that isn't clear to most people, as I believe it is, then I don't know where they've been for the last few years.
- John Pilger
Award Winning Journalist

It's only when journalists understand the role they play in this propaganda, it's only when they realize they can't be both independent, honest journalists and agents of power, that things will begin to change.

— John Pilger —

AZ QUOTES

BUT THE "EVIL RULING DEMONIC AUTHORITIES" PROMULGATE HATE LAWS FOR THEIR AGENDA AND SUPPRESS THE VOICE OF TRUTH!

JUDAISM IS NOT ZIONISM!

STATE OF ISRAEL IS "THE FIEFDOM OF ZIONIST" AND NOTHING TO DO WITH JUDAISM!

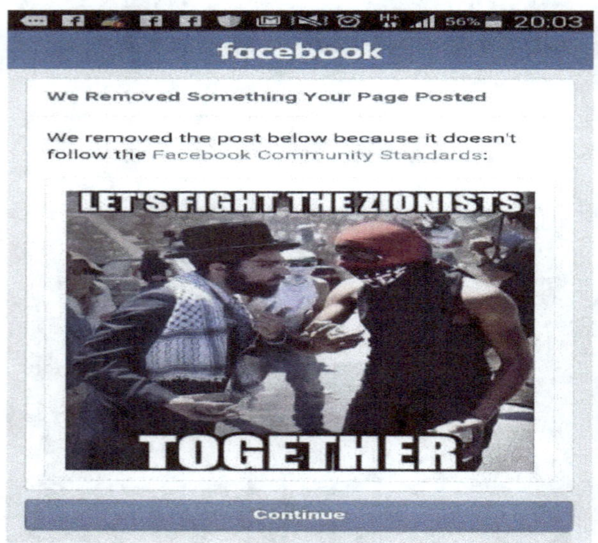

There are many "**peace loving Jews**" in the West and other parts of the world who **support the genuine cause of the Palestinians struggle for "freedom"** from the imposter Israeli regime. They also distinguish and **separate themselves** from "Zionism", who" lust for oppressive control and power", not over the **Palestinians but "worldwide"**!

PROPAGANDA CAMPAIGNS FOR WARMONGERING!

It is important to learn that why we see never ending "**wars and conflicts**", even after the creation of UNO in 1945, when states decided to resolve their conflicts at this forum and move toward "worldwide peace".

Firstly, this is because this organization is not meant to do this job! It has been created on **the property (plot) owned and donated by the Rockefellers (i.e. "the globalists", as mentioned above)**. These "psychopathic parasites" became financial powerful the in early 20th century, thereafter, **own the banking system, military industrial complex (industry), big pharma etc.** and "war is a profiteering business" for them!

Secondly, **Rothschilds** (main partner of Evil 13 Evil Families, mentioned above) had been engaged in creating and financing both sides of the conflicts since Napoleonic Wars till date! So, they always **lust for conflicts and planned them for depopulating the world, controlling the resources and off-course generating infinite amount of wealth!**

Just consider that USA got independence in 1776 and since then, there is **hardly few years** that it **has not been engaged** in any of "war and conflict", WHY???

Does any nation think of attacking USA (continent)? Are there any genuine adversaries or threats to USA? Answer: "NO". These parasites (mentioned above) create "pseudo enemies / adversaries" to deceive their public, so that "conflicts may be created" and they reap enormous benefits i.e. their demonic /satanist objectives mentioned above!!

Bottom line, there has been **no genuine "war" for last 250 years** or so between the nations, all are **engineered and pre-planned** (to serve the satanist interests of the psychopathic demonic parasites), even the World Wars and finally the upcoming **World War III, planned quite a while ago!!!**

THREE PSYCHOLOGICAL TECHNIQUES USED TO TAKE A COUNTRY / NATION TO WAR

1. Create the impression that the aggressor is actually acting in self-defence or defence of a helpless nation – provoking an enemy by exaggerating the danger posed by the enemy, WMDs, nuclear capability etc. (IRAQ)

2. Build up a crusade mythology, one that presents the aggressor as fighting for a higher moral ground like, spreading democracy, fighting terrorism, defending human rights etc. - (AFGHNISTAN)

3. De-humanize the enemy – islamophobia, human rights violator, racism etc. (SYRIA) .... Following with Iran, Russia, China, North Korea.....now

HOW USA / ZIONIST WAGED BIG WARS – FALSE FLAG OPERATIONS! – FEW EXAMPLES

USA on behalf of Zionists always go on war to serve the interest of the elite (bankers / capitalists)!!

- President William took USA to war with Spain – mysterious sinking of USS Maine in 1898

- Zionists plot the world war I – assassination of Archduke Franz Ferdinand of Austria in Sarajevo in summer of 1914

- President Wilson took USA to world war I – sinking of Lusitania (PASSENGER SHIP CARRYING ARMS & AMMUNITION FOR THE BRITISHERS) by Germans in 1915

- President Roosevelt took USA to world war II – Waiting for Pearl Harbour in 1941

- President Johnson took USA to war in Vietnam – False flag operation in Gulf of Tonkin (USS Maddox) in 1964

- And list goes on and on and on till date, the worst is 9/11, which lead to several false flag operations!!!

OVERTHROWING OTHER PEOPLE'S GOVERNMENTS: THE MASTER LIST

By William Blum

Instances of the United States overthrowing, or attempting to overthrow, a foreign government **since the Second World War**. *(* indicates successful ouster of a government)*

- China 1949 to early 1960s
- Albania 1949-53
- East Germany 1950s
- Iran 1953 *
- Guatemala 1954 *
- Costa Rica mid-1950s
- Syria 1956-7
- Egypt 1957
- Indonesia 1957-8
- British Guiana 1953-64 *
- Iraq 1963 *
- North Vietnam 1945-73
- Cambodia 1955-70 *
- Laos 1958 *, 1959 *, 1960 *
- Ecuador 1960-63 *
- Congo 1960 *
- France 1965
- Brazil 1962-64 *
- Dominican Republic 1963 *
- Cuba 1959 to present
- Bolivia 1964 *
- Indonesia 1965 *
- Ghana 1966 *
- Chile 1964-73 *
- Greece 1967 *
- Costa Rica 1970-71

- Bolivia 1971 *
- Australia 1973-75 *
- Angola 1975, 1980s
- Zaire 1975
- Portugal 1974-76 *
- Jamaica 1976-80 *
- Seychelles 1979-81
- Chad 1981-82 *
- Grenada 1983 *
- South Yemen 1982-84
- Suriname 1982-84
- Fiji 1987 *
- Libya 1980s
- Nicaragua 1981-90 *
- Panama 1989 *
- Bulgaria 1990 *
- Albania 1991 *
- Iraq 1991
- Afghanistan 1980s *
- Somalia 1993
- Yugoslavia 1999-2000 *
- Ecuador 2000 *
- Afghanistan 2001 *
- Venezuela 2002 *
- Iraq 2003 *
- Haiti 2004 *
- Somalia 2007 to present
- Honduras 2009 *
- **Libya 2011 ***
- **Syria 2012**
- Ukraine 2014 *

Q*:* Why will there never be a coup d'état in Washington?

A*:* Because there's **no American embassy there.**

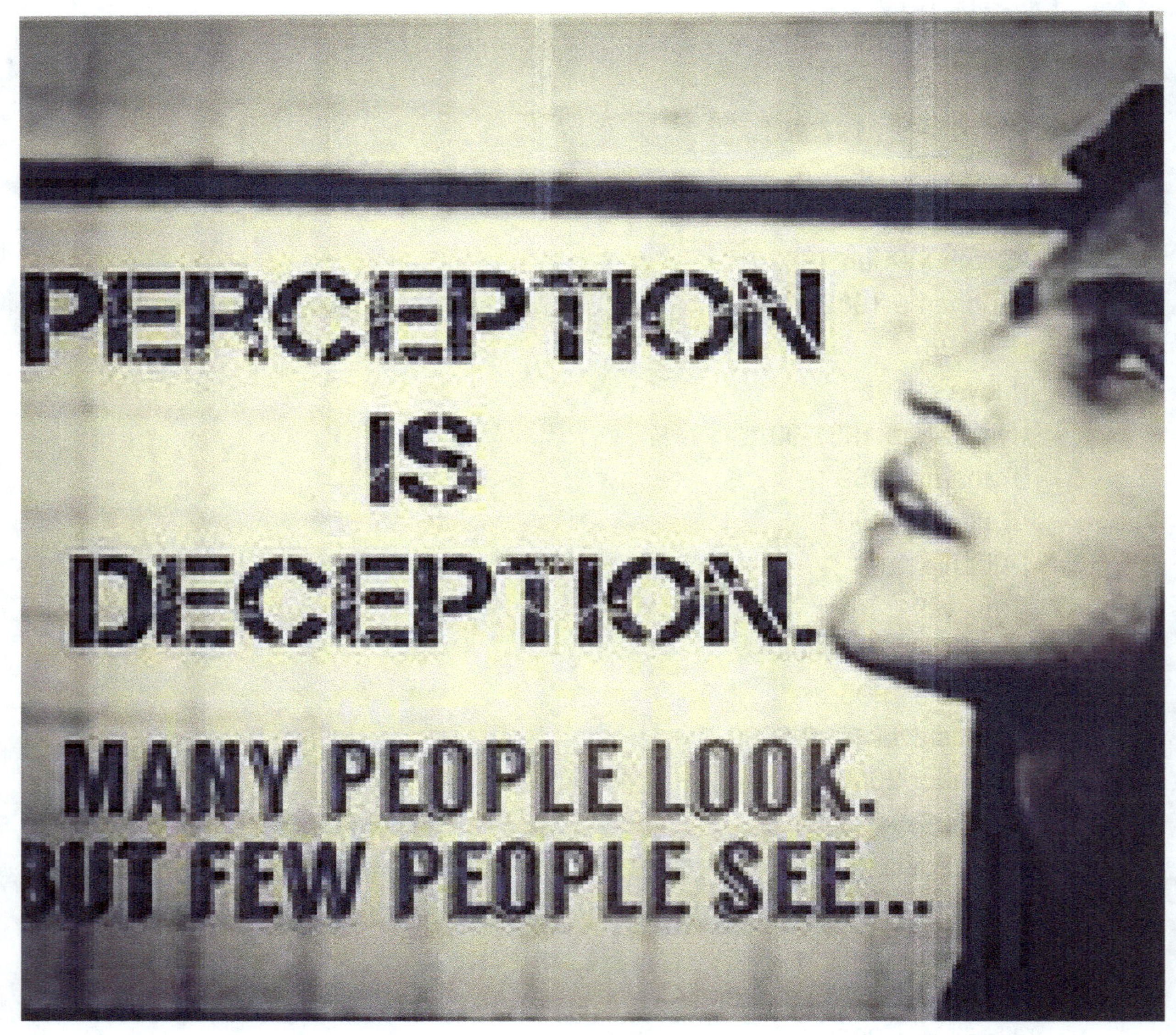

PERCEPTION
IS
DECEPTION.
MANY PEOPLE LOOK.
BUT FEW PEOPLE SEE...

THE WORLD IS INVERTED!!!

➢ **Perspective:** Democracy / Election is the best form of government

Actually: Dictatorship of the Capitalist / Bankers i.e. Banksters

➢ **Perspective:** War on Terror / Saviour for the Humanity

Actually: Promotion of agenda for colonizing the nations, keeping the military industrial complex flourishing

➢ **Perspective:** USA Economy is fine

Actually: Terrible downturn and almost collapsed (On a ventilator!)

➢ **Perspective:** Creation of Vaccines for controlling the viruses like aids, Ebola, Zika, Dengue etc.

Actually: Big time money making by the pharmaceuticals / massive depopulation / infertility programs

➢ **Perspective:** COVI19 / Coronavirus was a pandemic

Actually: All fake and manufactured fraud to lockdown people (house arrest), destroy economies (especially small and medium businesses worldwide), <u>earn billion dollars by big pharma, Bill Gates etc</u>, a steppingstone to ultimately control the people toward achieving One World Government!

➢ Perspective: **Mainstream media spreads the truth and mass education**

Actually: Medium of deception for brainwashing and mind controlling of masses to promote the evil elite agenda, <u>most powerful tool</u>!

➢ Perspective: **International Monetary System / Existing Credit based economy is workable for the mankind**

Actually: Fake, fraud, engineered, hyper inflated, system to enslave humanity and control natural resources across the world!

➢ Perspective: **Human Landing on Moon – Biggest achievement by mankind**

Actually: All fake, an MGM Studio production in 1969, NASA IS A TOTAL HOAX & biggest coverup, as it sucks billions of dollars of tax money per year for showing cartoons (fake science)!

➢ **Perspective:** Human Caused "<u>Global Warming</u>" is true science

Actually: A fraud engineered by Al Gore to promote Worldwide Carbon Taxation and Alternative Energy Sources at the behest of Evil Elite (to earn billions), under One World Agenda!

SO WATCH OUT!!

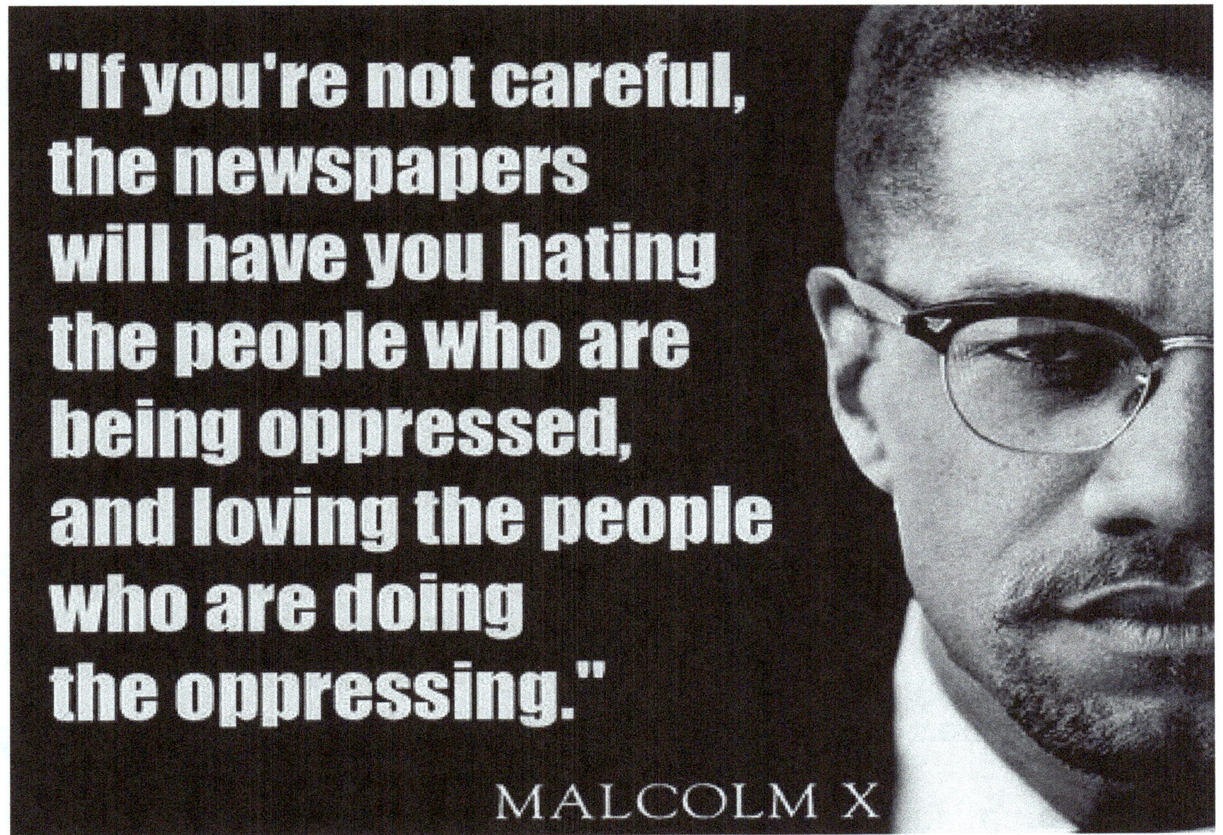

"If you're not careful, the newspapers will have you hating the people who are being oppressed, and loving the people who are doing the oppressing."

MALCOLM X

<u>**ALHAJ MALIK AL SHABAZ (MARTYR)– A GREAT PERSON (AFRO-AMERICAN LEADER) WHO COULD UNDERSTAND AND EXPOSE THE**</u> <u>**DECEPTION OF "DEMONIC ELITES" OBSESSED WITH THE MISSION TO ENSLAVE HUMANITY – POLITICALLY, SOCIALLY AND ECONOMICALLY!**</u>

THE GREAT RESET! - (UN AGENDA 2030 / 21st CENTURY)

(TOTAL WORLDWIDE CONTROL OF HUMANITY + RESOURCES)

- ❖ **One World Government**

- ❖ **One World Military**

- ❖ **One World Currency - Totally Digital!**

- ❖ **One World Bank**

- ❖ **One World Court**

- ❖ **Global Control of Regions (not countries) under UNO (core objective of its creation)**

- ❖ **Massive Depopulation via Wars, Viruses (biological warfare), Vaccines, Fukushima disaster, Poisoning water plants etc.**

- ❖ **Genetically Modified (GM) Foods [detrimental for health + modification of our genes] - Total Control of World Food (growth + trading), in addition to GM Organs (GMO's)**

- ❖ **Total Control Of Humanity** **Through Humanization Program (implanting microchip in humans) – Global Human Enslavement**

- ❖ **Enhancing The Role Of Artificial Intelligence (AI) in all spheres of life, wiring humans via internet and microchip, increased role of robotics, digitizing and automating every possible area**

- ❖ **Geo – engineering – modifying weather (weapon) via HAARP technology**

- ❖ **Social – engineering – via feminist revolution to destroy the family system and ultimately morality**

GLOBAL POLITICAL / GEO-POLITICAL CRISES

After establishing the basis of our "subject", we will now attempt to throw some light upon the **conflicts / wars** generally, but focussing our attention on the **Middle Eastern Region**, as it has been in turmoil for **more than thirty years and still on-going!**

A map was released by the Pentagon's in 2006 by Col. (Retd.) Ralph Peters (now a Congressman) proposing for reshaping the **Middle East Region** as follows:

<u>BEFORE</u>

BLOOD BORDERS – 2006

(PROPOSED)

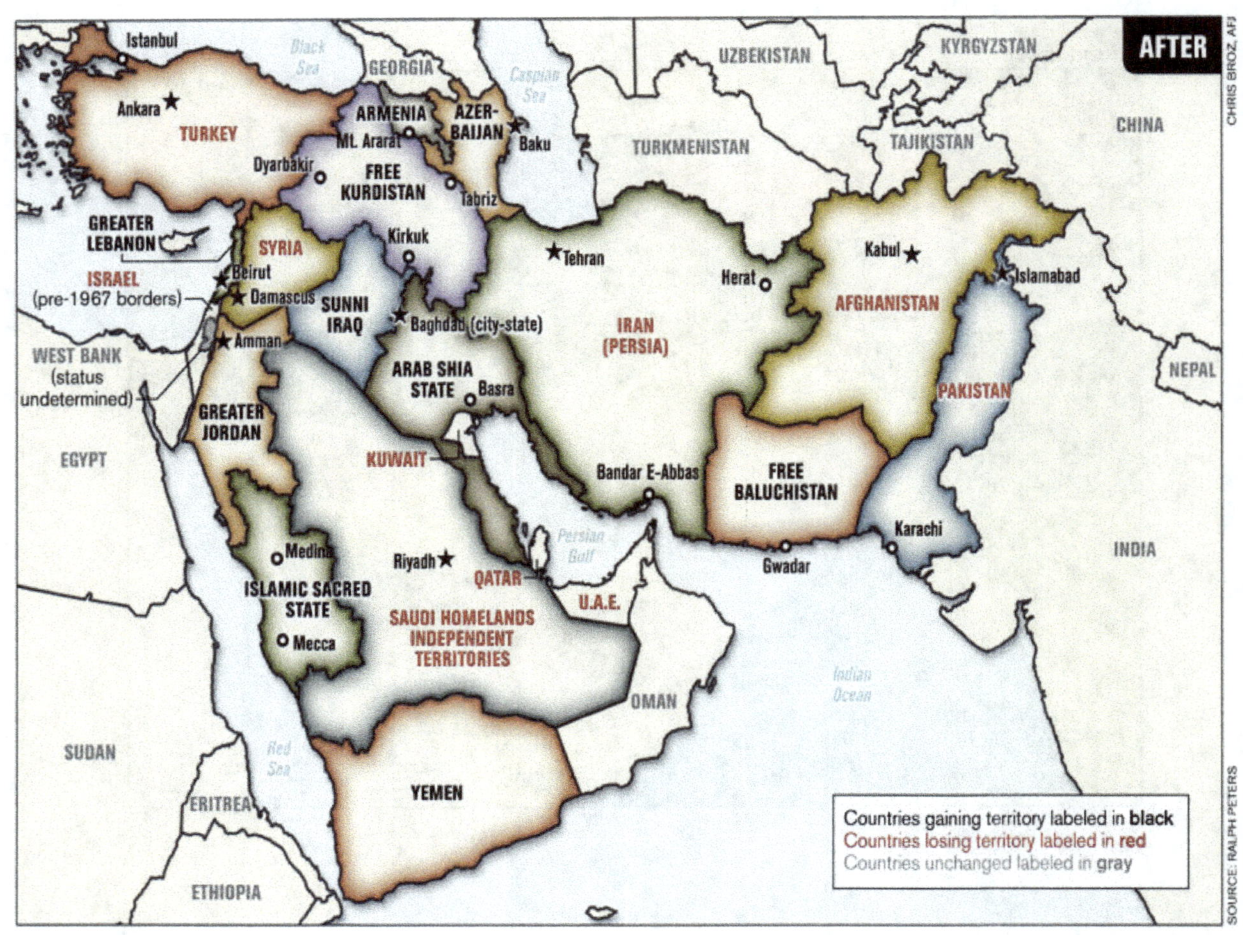

PRE-PLANNING – MIDDLE EAST

"... THE TRUTH IS THAT WE SHOULD HAVE GET RID OF SADAM HUSSAIN AND WE DIDN'T [THIS WAS AFTER SHIA UPRISING ENGINEERED BY CIA]. ONE THING WE LEARNT IS THAT WE CAN USE OUR MILITRY IN THE MIDDLE EAST, SO THAT SOVIET'S CAN'T STOP US. WE HAVE FIVE T0 TEN YEARS TO CLEANUP THOSE SOVIET CLIENTS / REGIME: SYRIA, IRAQ AND IRAN BEFORE NEXT SUPERPOWER COMES TO CHALLENGE US"– MEETING WITH UNDER SECRETARY PAUL WOLFOWITZ, PENTAGON - OPERATION DESERT SHIELD (IRAQ) 1991

"WE NEED TO TAKE OUT (SEVEN) 7 COUNTRIES IN FIVE (5) YEARS: IRAQ, "SYRIA", LEBANON, LIBYA, SOMALIA, SUDAN AND FINISHIG OFF WITH IRAN" –

SEPTEMBER 20, 2001, GENERAL WESLEY CLARK, SUPREME COMMANDER NATO FORCES DISCLOSED ABOUT A MEETING HELD AT PENTAGON BEFORE "9/11 ATTACK ON AFGHANISTAN"

<u>The Editor of "Philadelphia Trumpet" writes in its</u>

<u>monthly edition of August 2001 (a month before</u>

<u>9/11/2001):</u>

"The Last Crusade"

<u>"Most people think the crusades are a thing of the</u>

<u>past - over forever, but they are wrong. Preparations</u>

<u>are being made for the Final Crusade, and it will be the</u>

<u>bloodiest of all!"</u>

<u>AND THEN "9/11" HAPPEND, WHAT A SHEER</u>

<u>COINCIDENCE!!!</u>

USA ATTACKED IRAQ IN 2003 – OPERATION IRAQI FREEDOM

2001 – USA BUILT UP MASS PROPAGANDA CAMPAIGN THAT IRAQ HAS WEAPONS OF MASS DESTRUCTION (WMDs), 9/11 HAPPENED AND PLANNED TO ATTACK IRAQ ON 20/9/2001

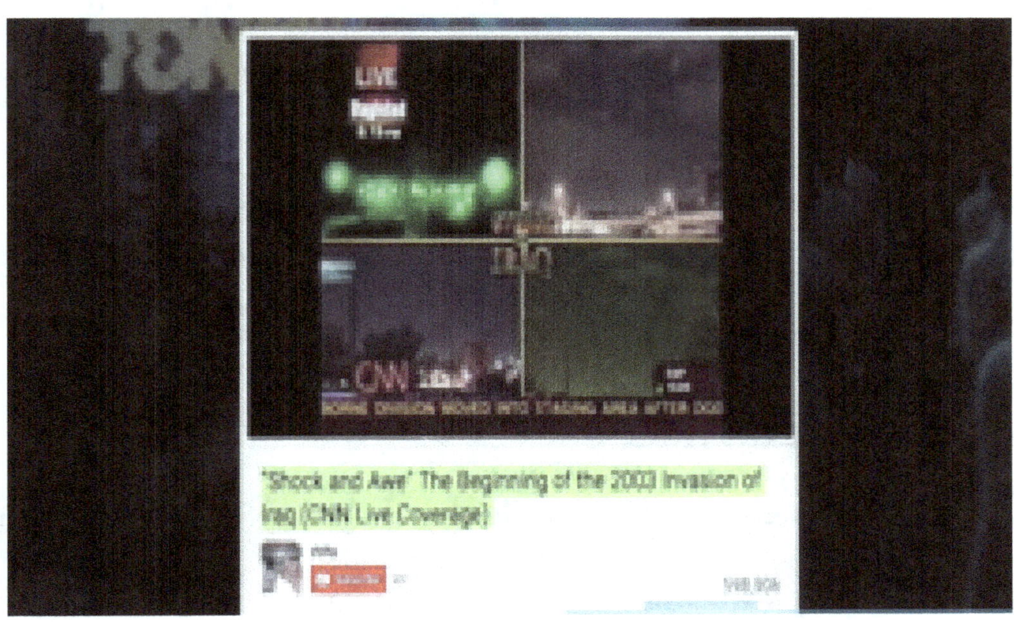

2003 – USA INVADED IRAQ [AFTER KILLING HUNDREDS OF THOUSANDS TILL DATE] AND ONCE AGAIN REVERT BACK TO PETRO-DOLLAR MONETARY SYSTEM [FROM EURO] AND BROUGHT THE IRAQI GOVERNMENT ON ITS KNEES!

THUS KEPT THE ZIONIST FEDERAL RESERVE BANKING SYSTEM IN POWER!!!

IN A BIGGER PICTURE, CONTROLLING IRAQ MEANS CONTROLLING ENERGY RESOURCES AND A STEP TOWARDS ESTABLISHING GREATER ISRAEL!

REGIME CHANGE THROUGH REBEL FIGHTERS IN LIBYA – WHY?

➢ Qaddafi **never opened** the **banking sector** for Western multi-national banks, besides Central Bank of Libya (CBL) allowed only handful of Islamic Banks were allowed!

➢ CBL is **not a member of Bank of International Settlements** that controls all central banks!!

➢ CBL **issues Libyan dinar** (gold coin) for its economy!!!!

➢ Qaddafi was devoted to the idea of **floating a 'gold dinar'** in conducting **international oil trade**. He **urged the OPEC members to re-price their oil in the gold dinar, instead of dollars.** His view **resonated well** with the **African Petro-economies**!

AGAIN Challenging Petro-Dollar Monetary System!!!

RESULT! TOPPLING OF QADDAFI REGIME AND DESTROYING ONCE A WELFARE NATION INTO DEBRIS BY THE US LED NATO ALLIANCE!!

Mohamed Al Magariaf, appointed leader after the death of Qaddafi
Spent 20 years in Atlanta where he planned the Libyan "regime change"
Said the attack on Benghazi was because the Libyans were convinced he was CIA
From Clinton E-Mail
imgflip.com

LIBYA BEFORE 2011 AND AFTER 2011???

Before Dignity
Operation

After Dignity
Operation

Before 2011
After 2011 NATO
Libya before NATO "Humanitarian Intervention"
Libya after NATO "Humanitarian Intervention"

Exclusive - Iran wants euro payment for new and outstanding oil sales - source

NEW DELHI | BY NIDHI VERMA

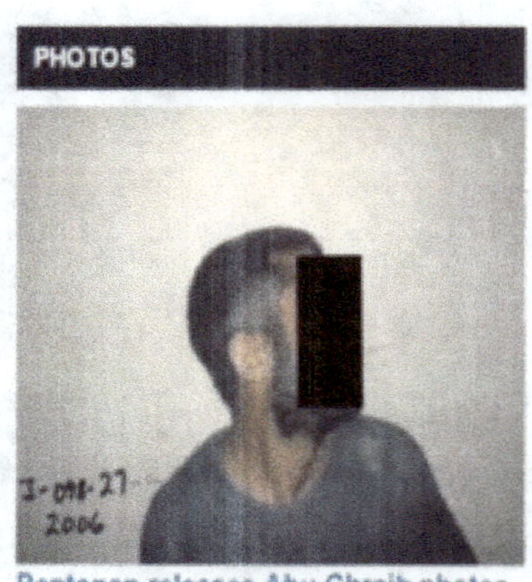

Pentagon releases Abu Ghraib photos

The Pentagon releases photographs linked to allegations of abuse of detainees in Iraq and Afghanistan.

Goodbye Petrodollar: Russia Accepts Yuan, Is Now China's Biggest Oil Partner

Russia reaps the rewards of dumping the dollar

SYRIAN CRISIS – A CASE STUDY

The geopolitical situation is an important subject to, as it linked to several neighbouring states like **Turkey, Iran, Kurds and Israel** and **under fire since 2011! We will try to understand its pros and cons in detail, as it led to several other manufactured issues that affected Europe and USA!**

Imagine the Current situation of Syria!

- ❖ **A piece of land disrupted and destroyed since 2011...**
- ❖ **About 22 million population, size little more than State of North Dakota (USA)**

Where.....

- ❖ **USA - bombing**

- ❖ **France - bombing**

- ❖ **Israel - bombing**

- ❖ **Kurds - bombing**

- ❖ **USA backed rebels (FSA, Al Nusra, Al Qaeda)- bombing**

- ❖ **ISIS - bombing**

- ❖ **Turkey – bombing**

- ❖ **Russia is bombing (Support of Syrians)**

- ❖ **Britain is bombing**

- ❖ **Iran's military presence (fighting with Syrians)**

- ❖ **China not yet, but is about to involve on side with Russia (if requested)**

WHO IS BEHIND SYRIAN CRISIS?

SAME TECHNIQUE FOR REGIME CHANGES IN LIBYA WAS REPEATED!

OBJECTIVE!

USA EXPOSED!

A Syrian pro-government protester shouts slogans during a protest following Friday prayers outside the Omayyad Mosque in Damascus, Syria, Friday, April 15, 2011.   AP PHOTO/MUZAFFAR SALMAN

ARMS SHIPMENT FOR "MODERATE / REBELS / TERRORIST" IN SYRIA?

GEO-POLITICS BEHIND THE SCENES

WIKI LEAKS – USA LED SAUDI, QATAR, AND TURKEY SECRET DEAL AGAINST SYRIAN GOVERNMENT IN 2012

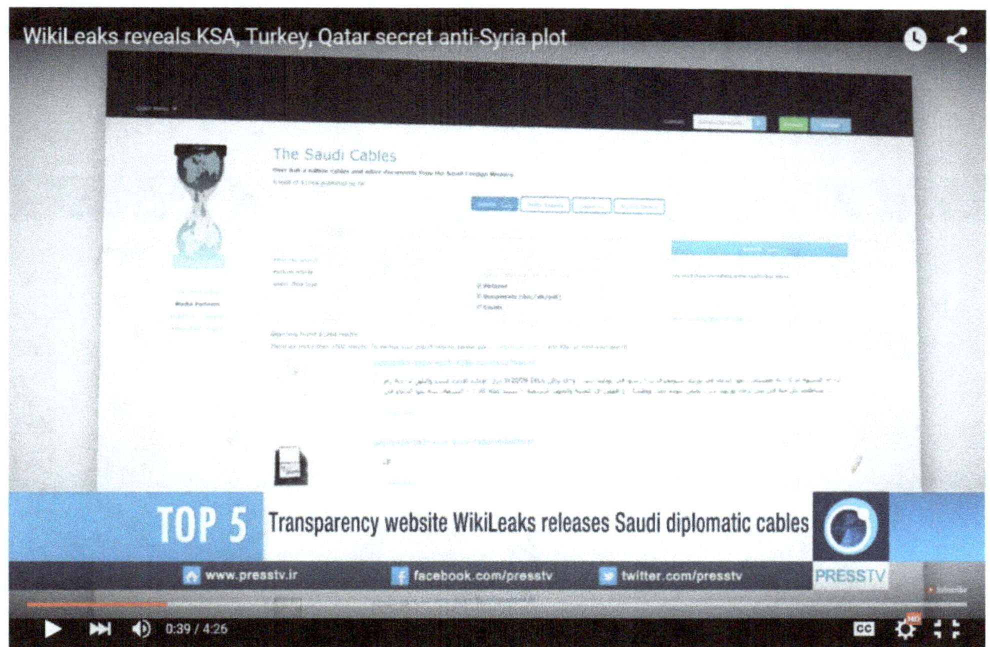

CIA TRAINING THE SYRIAN REBELS IN JORDAN!

GAS PIPLINE POLITICS (GEO-POLITICS CONVERGES WITH ECONOMY)

<u>IN 2014 – EU CONCLUDED THAT 42% OF THEIR NATURAL GAS IS IMPORTED FROM RUSSIA – MAY BE A STRATEGIC THREAT!</u>

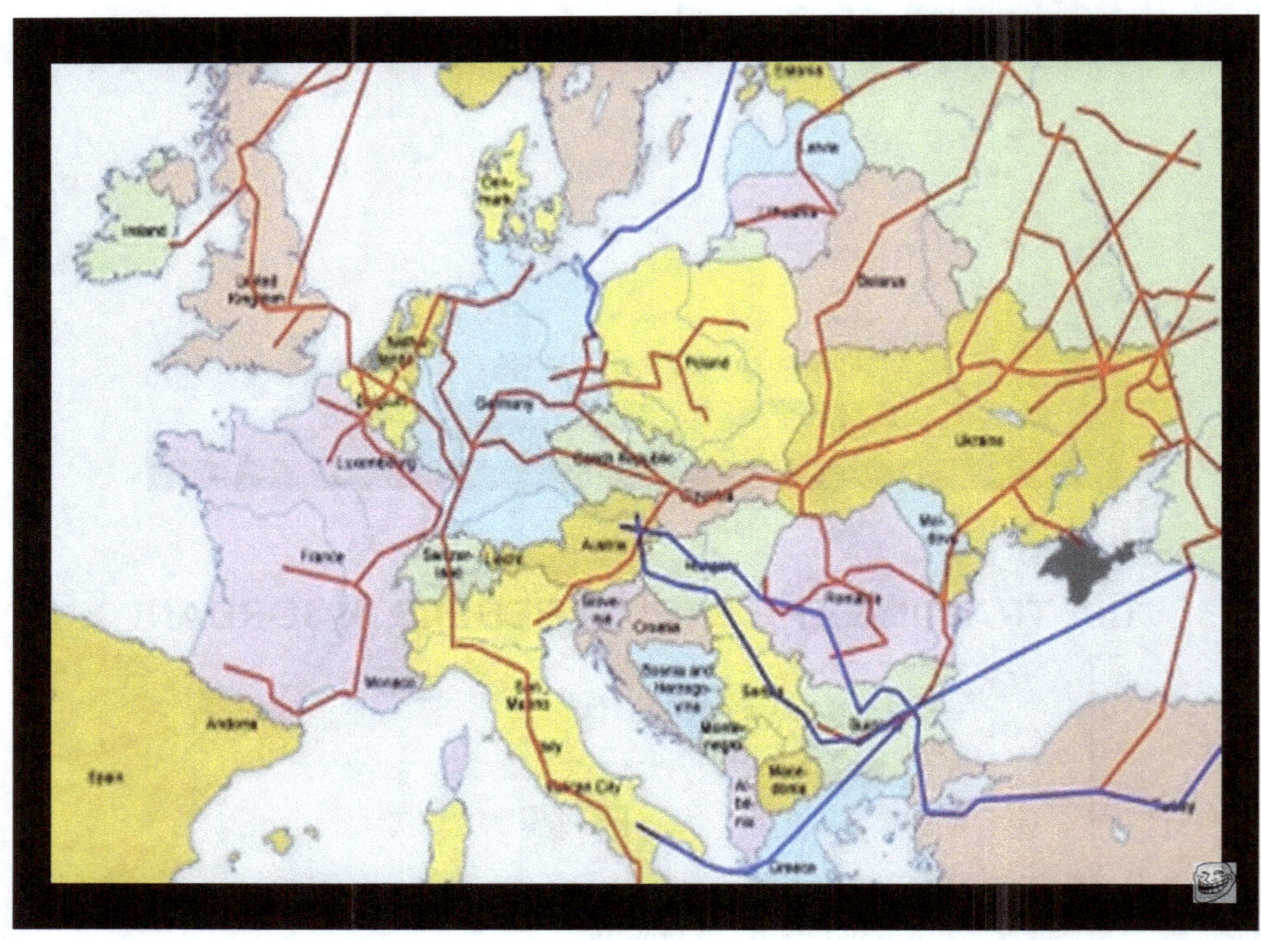

<u>BELOW IS THIS IS THE WORLD'S LARGEST KNOWN GAS RESERVE</u> IN THE WORLD, THAT CAN MEET THE <u>EU NEEDS AND RUSSIA KNOWS THIS!</u> BUT WHEN IRAN AND CHINA IS INVOLVED THEN IT IS A DIFFERENT BALL GAME!!

WORLD'S LARGEST KNOWN GAS RESERVE IN THE WORLD IN THE AREA SHARED BY IRAN AND QATAR!

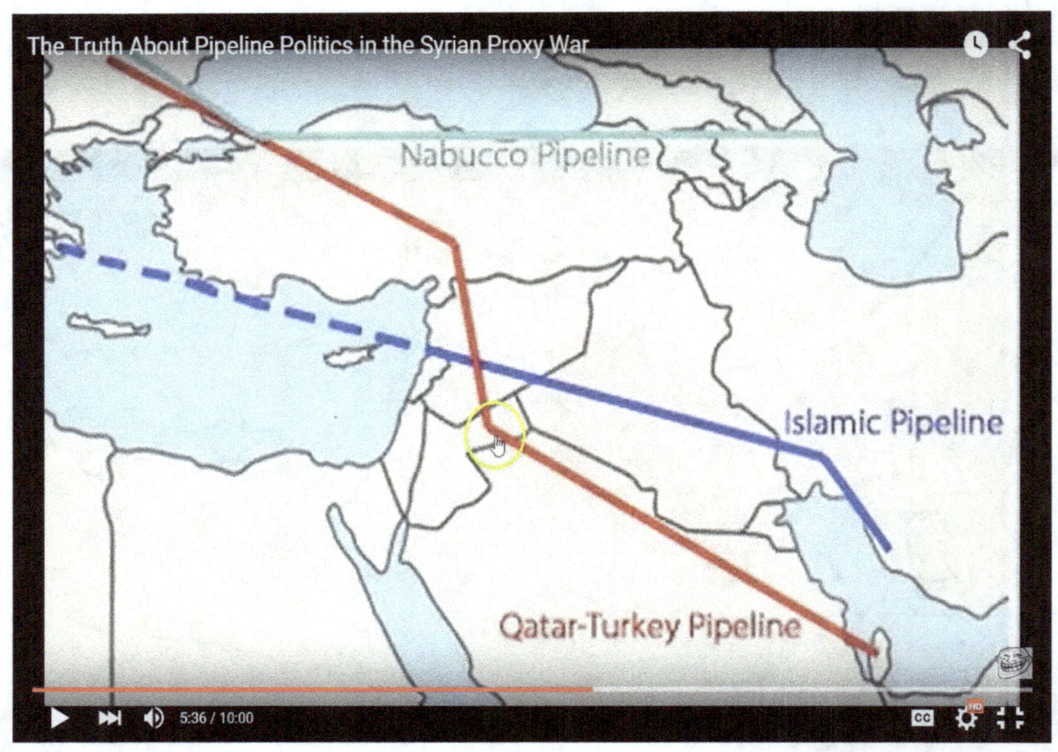

NATO [TURKEY] + SAUDI ARABIA TRAINED ISIS FIGHTERS

IN THE FOOTHILLS OF JORDAN TO DESTABILIZE

"NORTHEN SYRIA" AFTER CREATING HAVOC IN "IRAQ"

<u>**OBJECTIVES:**</u>

- ➢ **TO ENSURE THE <u>NORTHERN PART OF SYRIA REMAINS DISTURBED AND AN ETRNAL WARZONE FOR SABOTAGING "ISLAMIC PIPELINE"!</u> ALTERNATIVELY, <u>QATAR – TURKEY PIPELINE</u> SHOULD BE <u>SUPPORTED AND PROMOTED (VESTED INTEREST)</u>, WHICH HAS TO PASSTHROGH <u>NORTHERN SYRIA!</u>**

- ➢ **TO ALLOW GAIN CONTROL OF "<u>TREMDOUS QUANTITIES OF "PETROLEUM" IN GOLAN HEIGHTS REGION"</u> BY THE <u>ISRAELIS</u>.**

How The 'Problem-Reaction-Solution' Paradigm Works

1. The government creates or exploits a problem then attributes blame to others

2. The populace reacts by asking the government for protection and help to solve the problem

3. The government offers the solution that was planned by them long before the crisis occurred

Outcome: Rights and liberties are exchanged for the Illusion of protection and help

LIKE 9/11, EBOLA, AIDS, ZIKA, CORONA / COVID19 (MANUFACTURED VIRUSES), MARTIAL LAW, VACCINATION PROGRAMS, WARS, PLANDEMICS, ETC. ALL ARE MANUFACTURED TO FORWARD THE HIDDEN AGENDA TO CONTROL POPULATION AND MOVE TOWARDS ONE WORLD GOVERNMENT, "MIGRANT CRISIS" WAS ALSO ENGINEERED!

SYRIAN MIGRANT CRISIS

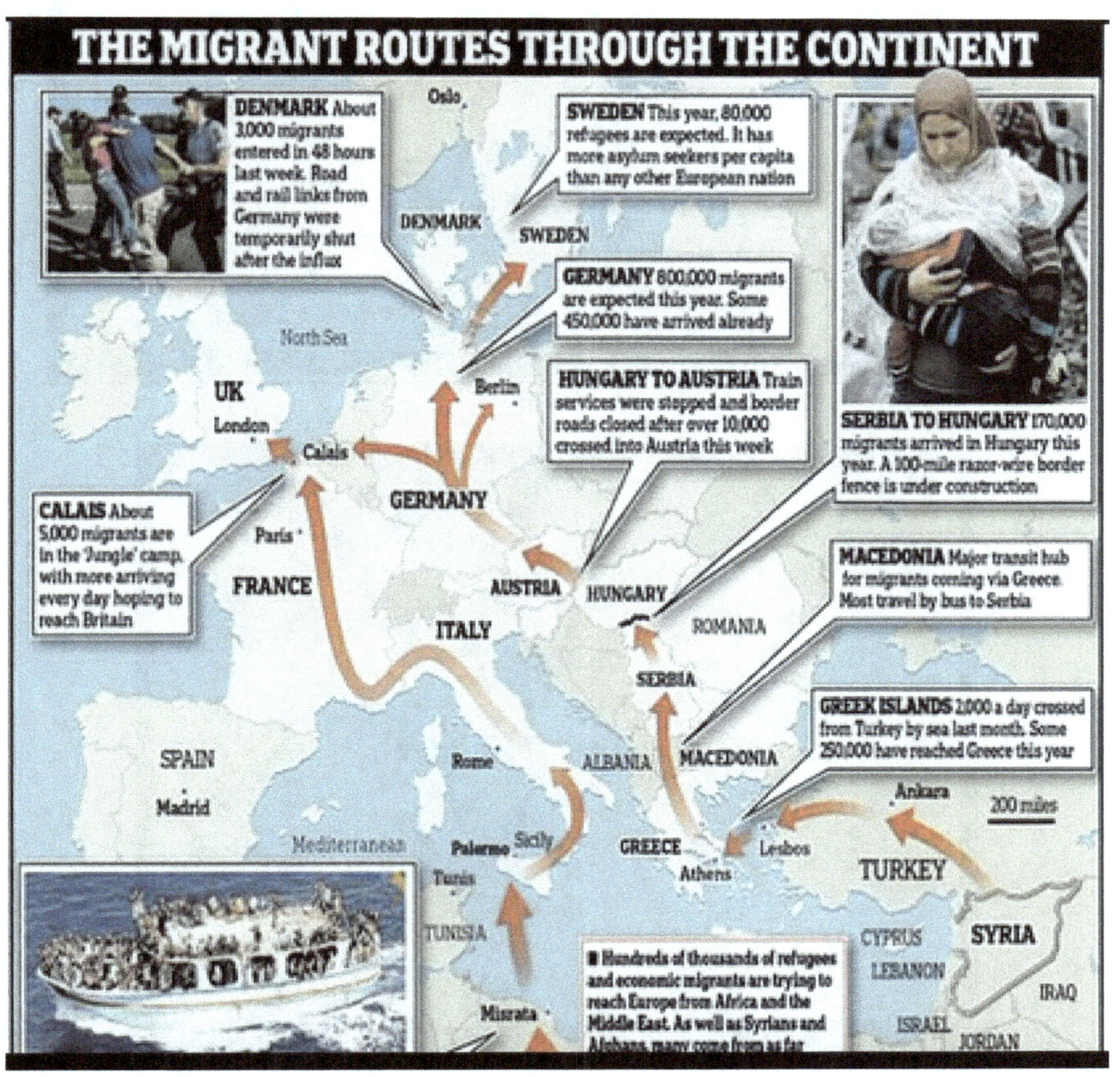

WAS IT RANDOM OUT OF CHAOS, DEFNITELY NOT!

RATHER ENGINEERED BY GEORGE SOROS!

WATCH THIS!

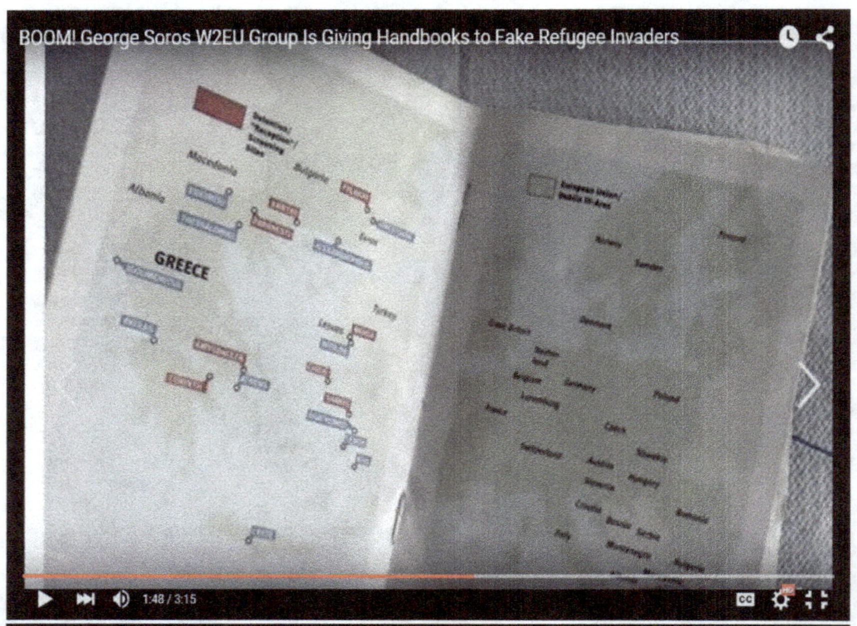

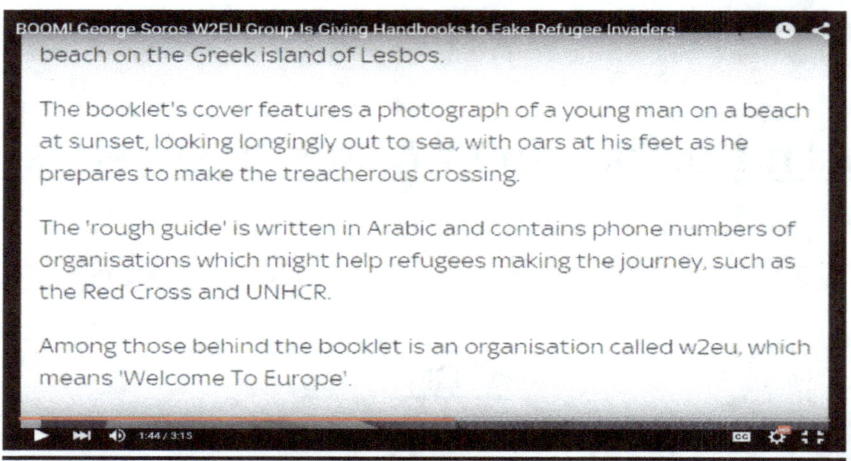

beach on the Greek island of Lesbos.

The booklet's cover features a photograph of a young man on a beach at sunset, looking longingly out to sea, with oars at his feet as he prepares to make the treacherous crossing.

The 'rough guide' is written in Arabic and contains phone numbers of organisations which might help refugees making the journey, such as the Red Cross and UNHCR.

Among those behind the booklet is an organisation called w2eu, which means 'Welcome To Europe'.

This scam has also been confirmed the Head of EU Frontier Police!!

These Pass Ports were for sale @USD 1,500 in Turkey. People of different nations are buying in multiples to seek asylum in Europe for economic reasons!

9 out of 10 refugees from Macedonia claimed to be Syrians!!!

Where was it leading too??

ULTERIOR MOTIVES OF ENGINEERED MIGRANT CRISIS

- **To promote 'antisemitism' in Europe and America, so that Jews will be driven out of Europe and America and into Greater Israel!**

- **To inculcate fear among Europeans and create Police State-like situations in European countries and total control (as in USA) by introducing terrorists/ ISIS in garb of refugees. This has been an objective of Zionists (George Soros)!**

- **To destroy the European nationalism / identity, culture and borders for moving toward multi-ethnic society [European zone] in order to enforce global agenda - "one world government"**

- **But this does not mean that there is no suffering for the poor Syrians. Another objective of this psyop is to make an excuse for continuing the bombing of citizens of Syria in the cover of ISIS, Kurds or Assad's army. Zionists just want to finish them off and send the rest away as refugees so that Syria will be empty as possible before Israel 'occupies' it**

- **The poor people of Syria were caught by the devil (ISIS, Saudi Arabia, Turkey alliance backed by USA / Zionists!**

ROLE OF KEY STAKEHOLDERS

ROLE OF TURKEY, QATAR & SAUDI ARABIA

☐ **TURKEY – NATO ALLY**

Modern day Turkey continues its **alliance with Zionists & Western Christians through NATO** and has been complicit in every evil design of NATO.

Turkey has **taken part in every Zionist-led operation of NATO** including Iraq, Afghanistan, Libya, Tunisia and now Syria; and that too wilfully without any inch of regret, just to please its Western masters; in this way it continues to do much harm to the Muslim Ummah / Community.

☐ **TURKEY & SAUDI ARABIA JOINT ROLE IN FORMATION / SUPPORTING OF ISIS AND FSA**

Probably **Serena Shim** (journalist) was **murdered for exposing how weapons were provided to ISIS, which arrived at Incirlik Airbase (Turkey) and how "ISIS terrorists" being smuggled from Turkey along with heavy weapons and logistic support into Syria.**

<u>ISIS earned around $ 50 Million per month by selling oil "cheaply" to the Son of Turkey's President Erdogan</u> (by <u>stealing Syrian's Oil)</u>, which was seriously damaged by Russian air strikes, that is why they entered their ground troops in coalition with US to establish "**<u>Secured Zone</u>**" along **<u>Kurdish border (a narrow opening to support IS / FSA / Rebels etc.)!!</u>**

<u>SAUDI – QATAR – TURKEY STRATEGIC CONCEIVED PIPLE LINE PROJECT FOR SUPPLYING GAS TO EUROPE</u> (<u>BUT REQUIRED REGIME CHANGE IN SYRIA</u>) **AND THEY BECAME PARTNERS IN CRIME TO INVADE SYRIA   - <u>OFFCOURSE WITH NATO BACKING UP!!!</u>**

ROLE OF RUSSIA, IRAN & CHINA

- Russia is an ally of Syria , while Iran has treaty with Syria

- **Assad's resistance** against **<u>Saudi-Qatar-Turkey pipeline</u>** goes in favour of Russia, thus defended him with full force!

- Russia targeted both ISIS and all US / NATO strategic ground assets prepared during 4 years for destabilizing the regime - a surprise and **timely checkmate to US / NATO plans!**

- Iran being a strategic ally of Syria is actively fighting with boots on ground alongside Assad

- China has allied with Russia for defending Assad and developing strategic ties with Iran – Emerging Eastern World Order!

Can we expect some serious military conflicts in the region? Off course!

THE GREAT GAME FOR THE END GAME!

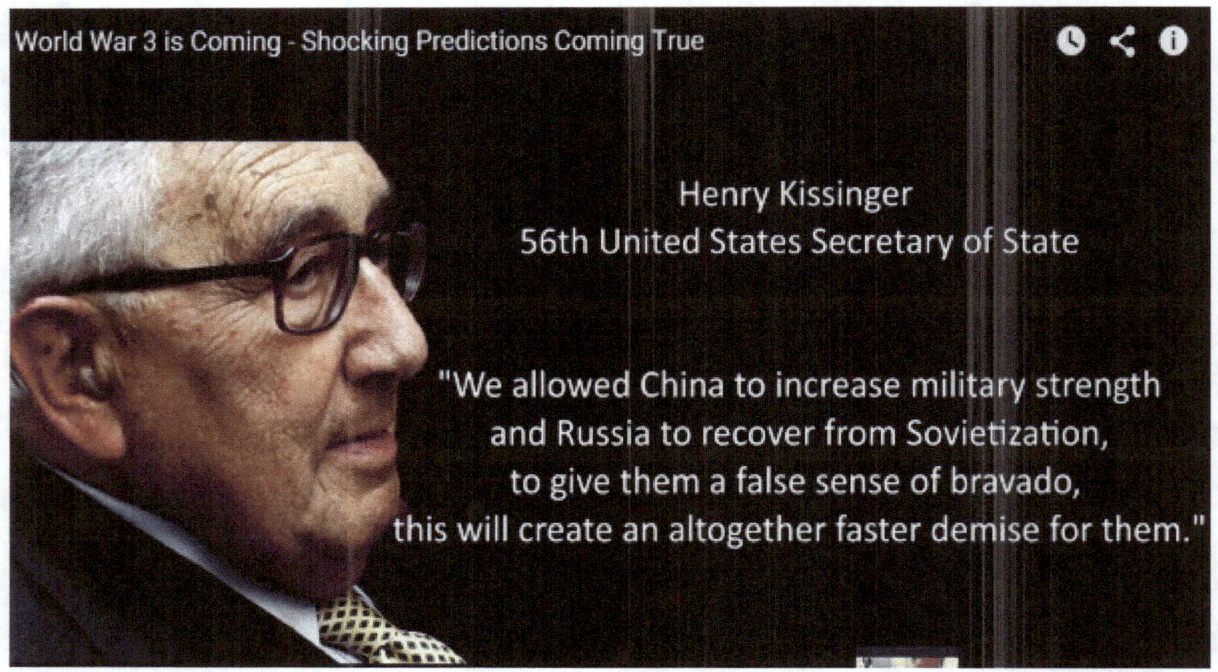

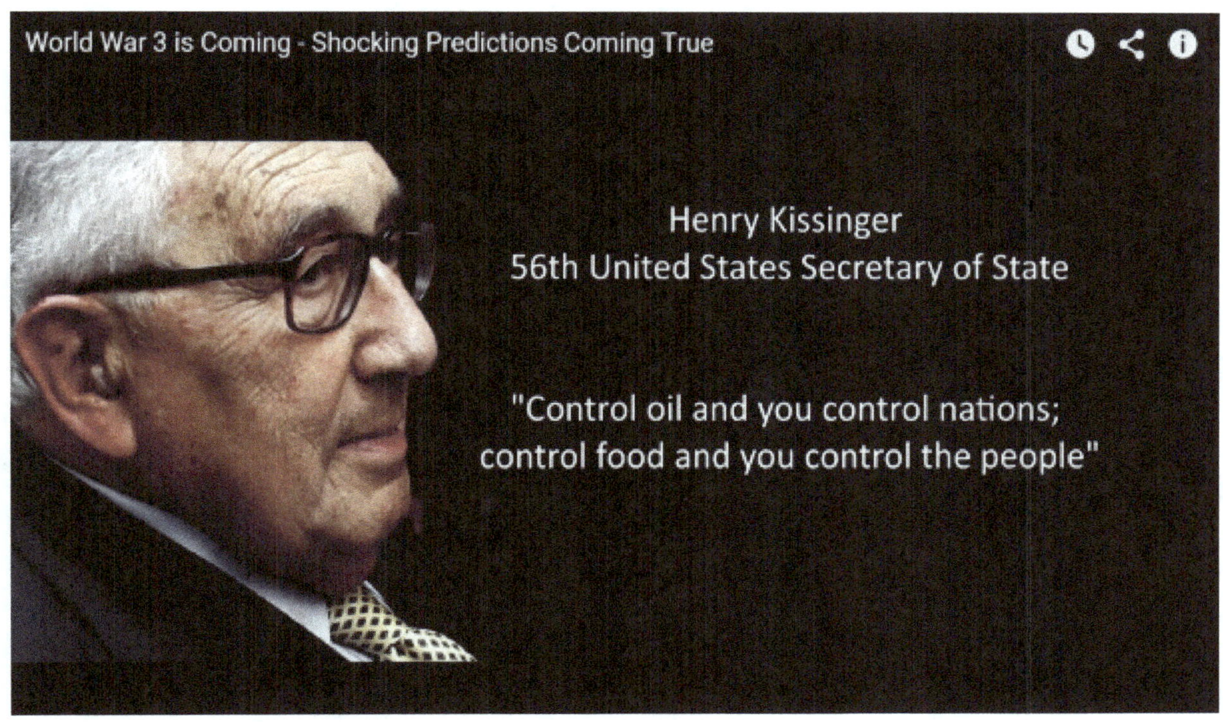
Henry Kissinger
56th United States Secretary of State

"Control oil and you control nations;
control food and you control the people"

4 STAR GENERAL WESLEY CLARK

"...TAKE OUT 7 COUNTRIES IN 5 YEARS: IRAQ, SYRIA, LEBANON, SUDAN, SOMALIA AND IRAN"

"...PRESENCE OF PETROLEUM WAS ONE OF THE KEY FACTORS OF REGIME CHANGE BY THE GREAT POWER FOR USING BRUTE FORCE IN THE REGION....."

General (R) Wesley Clark, NATO Supreme Commander

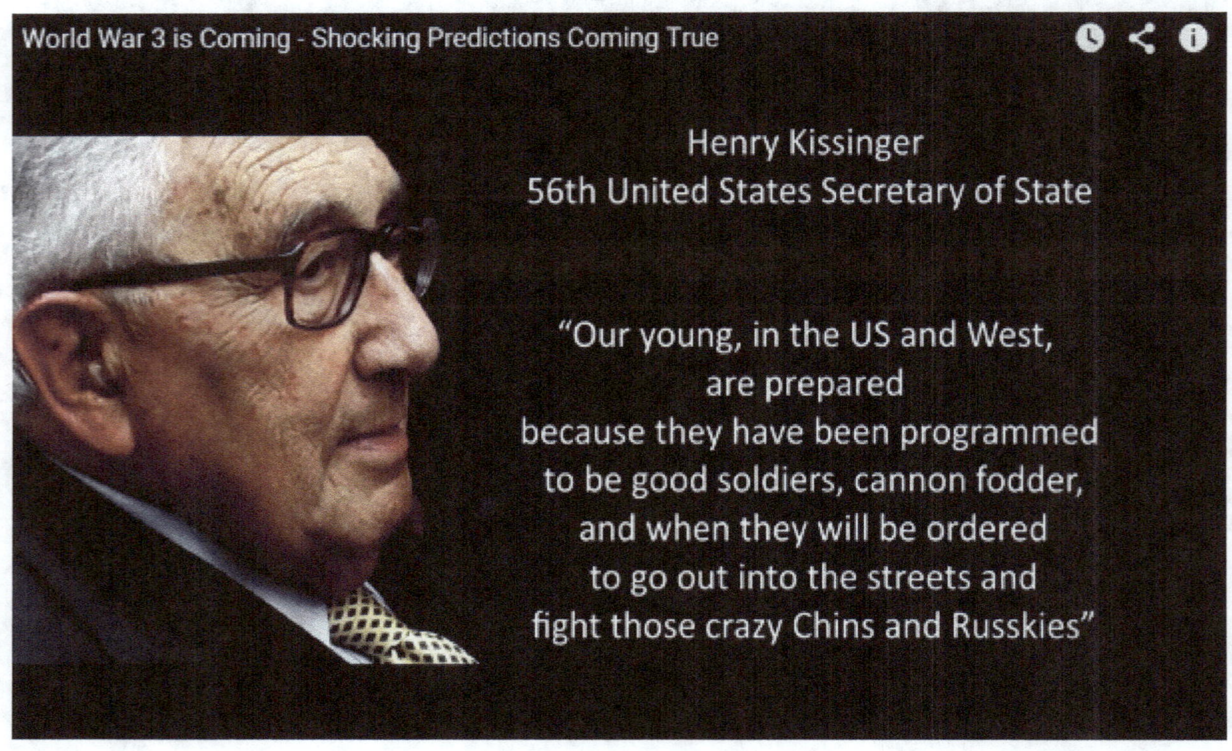

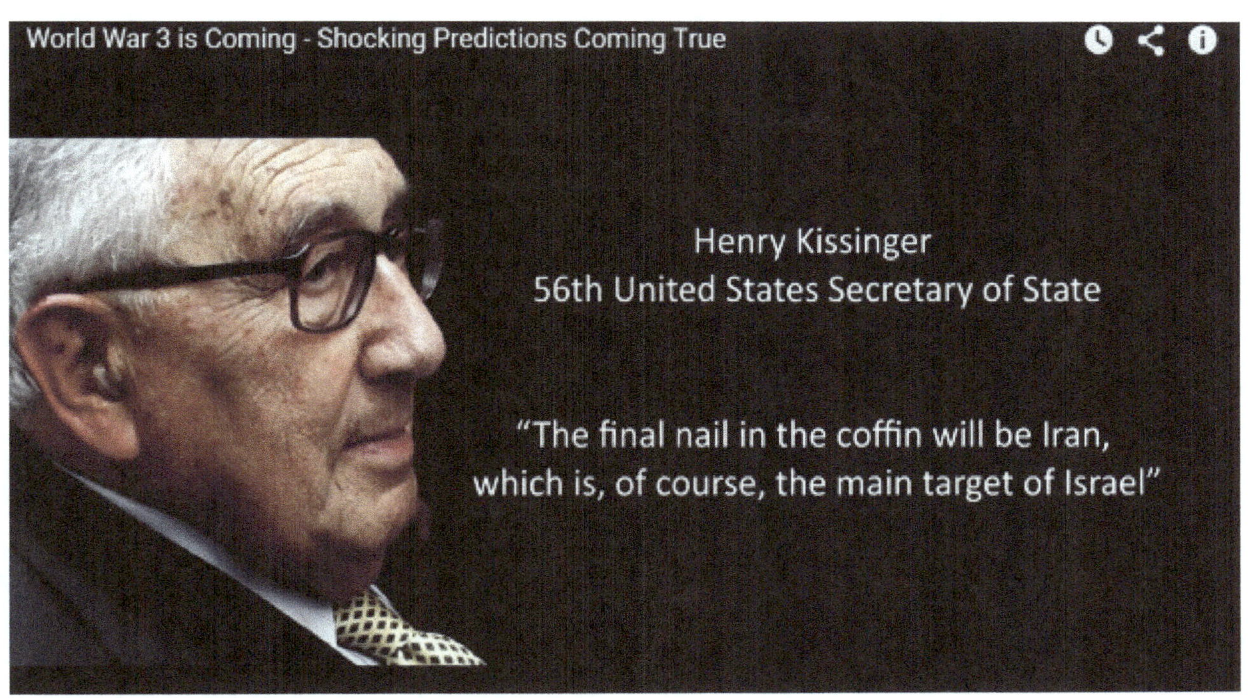

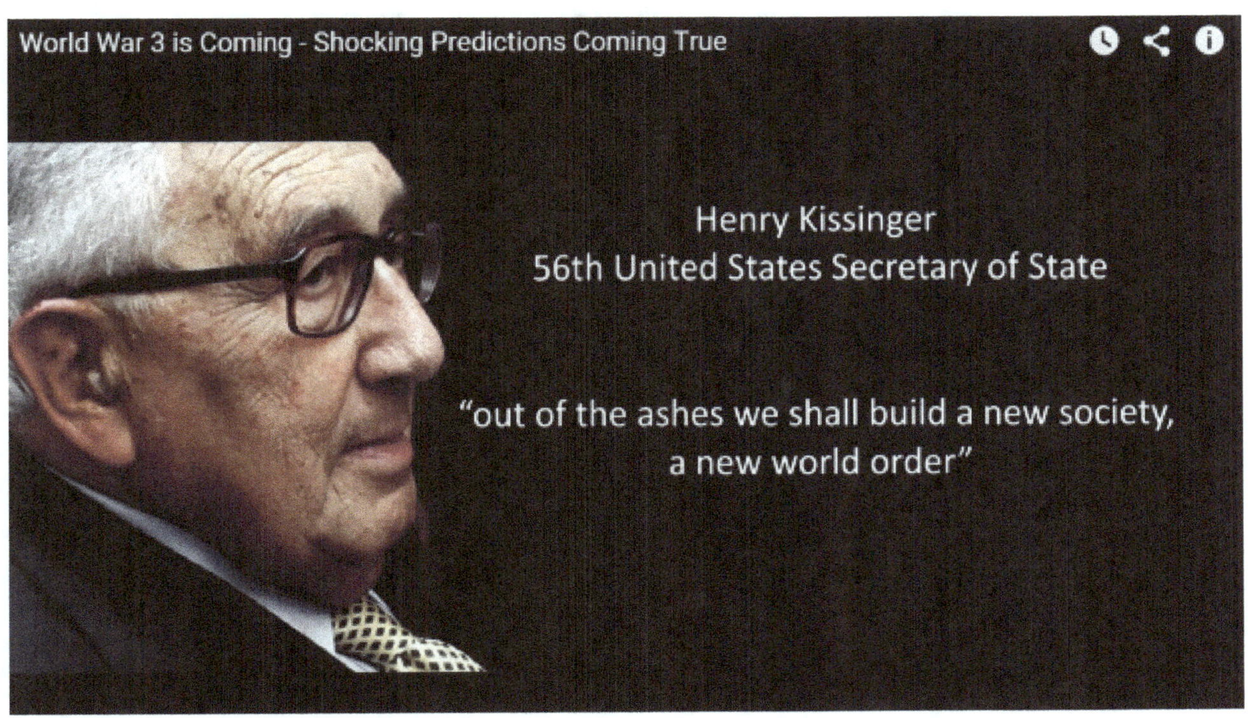

<u>NEW WORLD ORDER MAP</u>

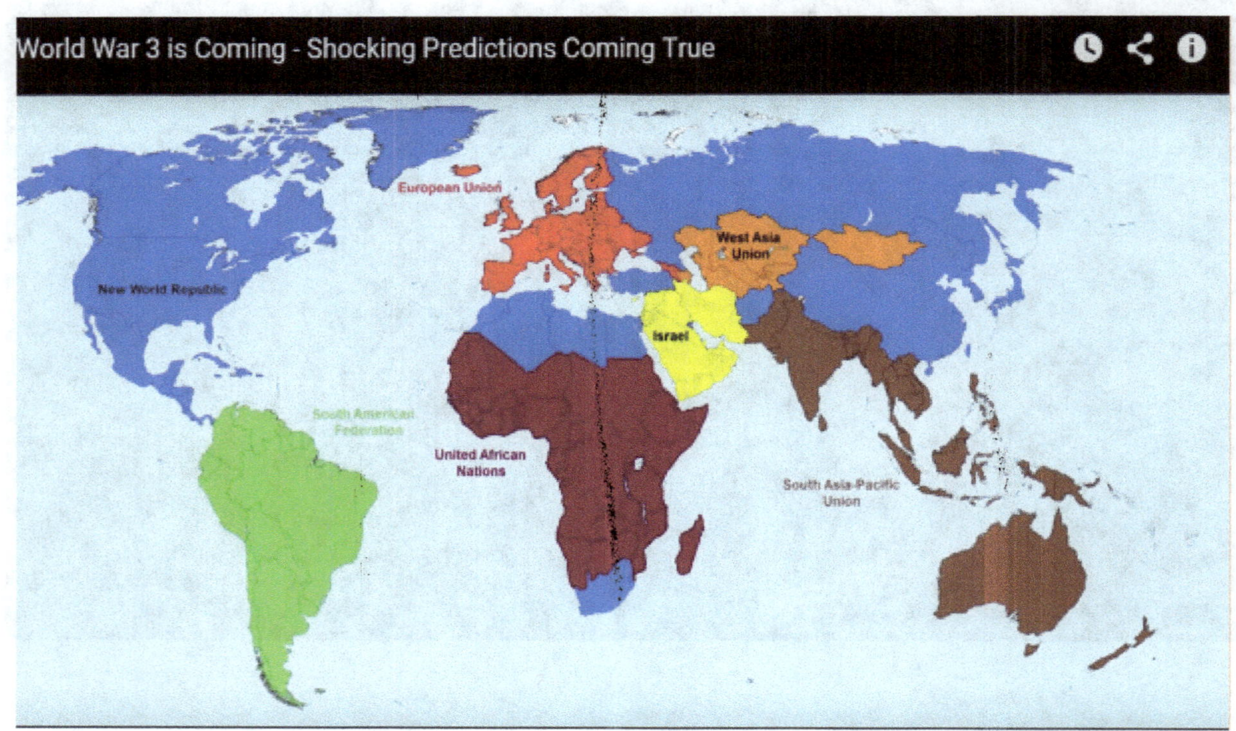

THIS WAS PLANNED IN 1897!!!

PROTOCOLS OF ELDERS OF ZION

GLOBAL AGENDA

- ❖ **Establishment** of **global godless civilization** based on **secularism (politics based on fraudulent popular democracy) –** **Done!**

- ❖ **Controlling of <u>global economy</u> through capitalism based on <u>**interest based exploitative / oppressive banking and monetary systems**</u> (fraudulent paper currency without gold / silver backing) –** **Done!**

- ❖ **Feminist Revolution -** **Propagating vulgarity, LGBT Culture, Satanism, Demonic Cults by all possible means** **(to destroy the decent social system across all civilizations) – <u>almost done, with traces of resistance!</u>**

REGIONAL AGENDA:

- ❖ **Launching of <u>**Armageddon to reshape the Middle East map**</u>, take <u>down big powers like USA and Russia for the creation of Greater Israel</u> –** **final preparations are underway before our eyes!**

- ❖ **Destroying of <u>**Al Aqsa and Dome of Rock Mosques**</u>**

- ❖ **Construction of <u>3rd Temple</u> in Bait Al Maqdas /Jerusalem!**

- ❖ **Placement of the <u>Throne of David</u> (currently in Westminster Abbey Church) in the 3rd Temple**

- ❖ **Restoration of Israel as the Ruling State of the World –** <u>Quite near to achieving this</u> Ultimate goal!

IS THE WWIII APPROACHING?

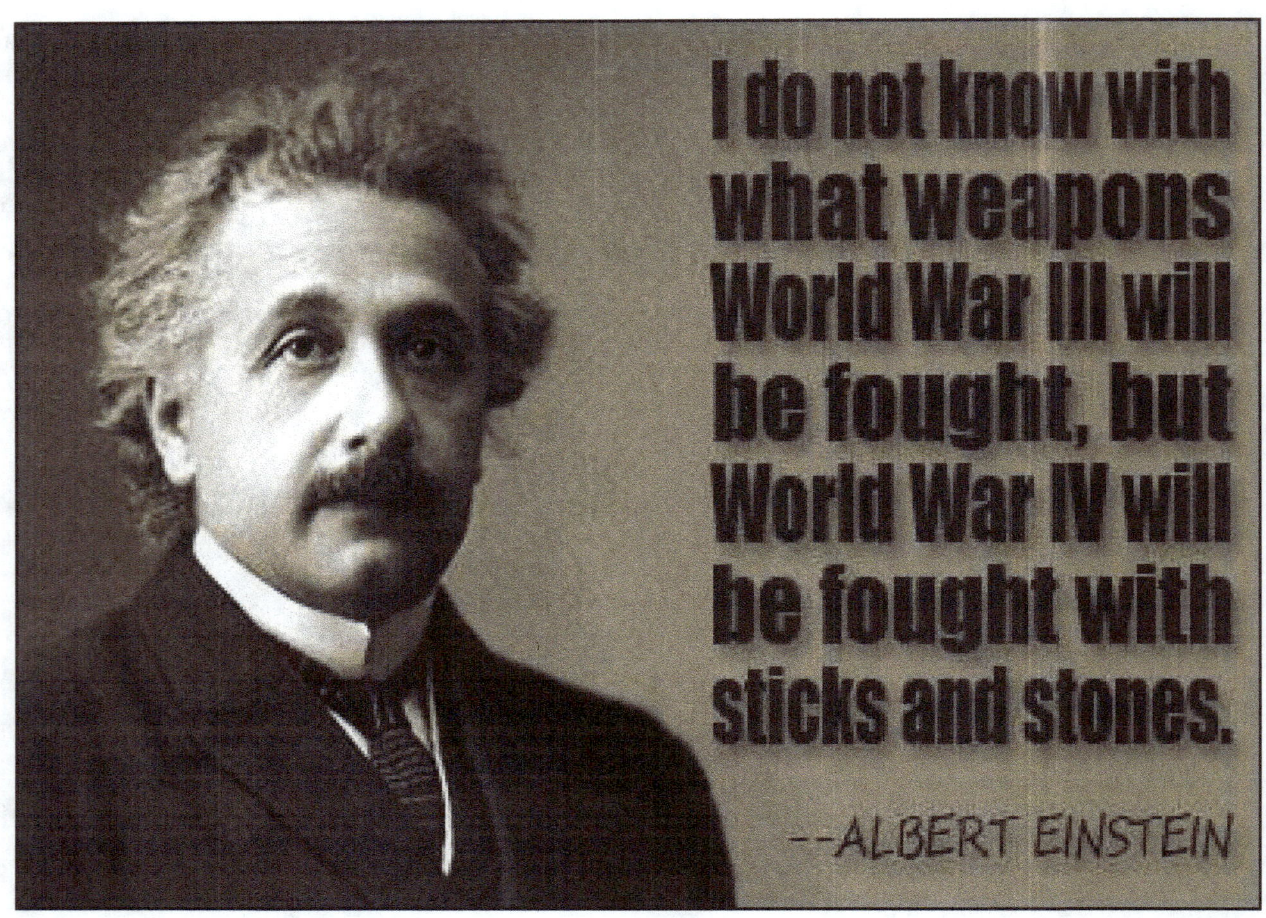

TRIGGERS FOR WWIII (IMMINENT DANGERS)

❖ The more USA / NATO gets desperate to overthrow Assad (Syrian President on the behest of Israel), Russia gets more involved and dominant!

❖ With everyday gaining of Russia's strategic control in Middle Eastern Affairs, Petro-dollar is challenged! China – Russia –iron has almost de-pegged themselves from Petro-dollar trade!!

❖ **US led NATO's adventure** to Escalate War between Ukraine Russia!

❖ **Escalation of NATO and Russian military activities around the Baltic States (Latvia, Lithuania, Estonia)**

❖ Recently, Russia has sent its **Nuclear Submarine and Destroyer Ships** loaded with "Nuclear Warheads" for patrolling from **North Sea to cover one third of world i.e. Atlantic and Pacific! This is done after the announcement of NATO for the inclusion of Finland and Sweden! Actually, it is a clear message to USA (neighbouring Russia).**

❖ **China's increased dominance in South China sea is considered as a strategic threat to US and its Allies!**

COLLAPSE OF US DOLLAR - A MAJOR SIGN!

- **Collapse of USD is imminent due to global decline in value and need of dollar! Of course, it is a "fake / fraudulent" paper** currency created by Federal Reserve Private Bank (Axil of Evil for prevailing International Monetary System, **without "any sort of backing** by gold or silver", which is <u>Real / Sound / Sunnah money!!</u>

- **US Debt crossing USD 31.4 Trillion,** and this artificial "<u>Giant Bubble" is bound to collapse</u>, rather engineered to be collapsed in very near future!

- The current status of USD is "Petro-Dollar", therefore with the collapse of USD, petroleum the neediest commodity will inflate "skyrocketing", therefore cause global "hyperinflation" and chaos and possible trigger WWIII!!

- As the USD loses its status of "<u>World Reserve Currency</u>", therefore all those <u>countries who maintain USD Reserves for obvious reasons are bound to collapse</u>!

- Major economic giants like <u>China, Russia are moving away from the US Dollar and dumping their USD based Assets in the market.</u> Formation of <u>BRICS and Asia Infrastructure Investment Bank (China) are <u>challenging the US Dollar!</u></u>

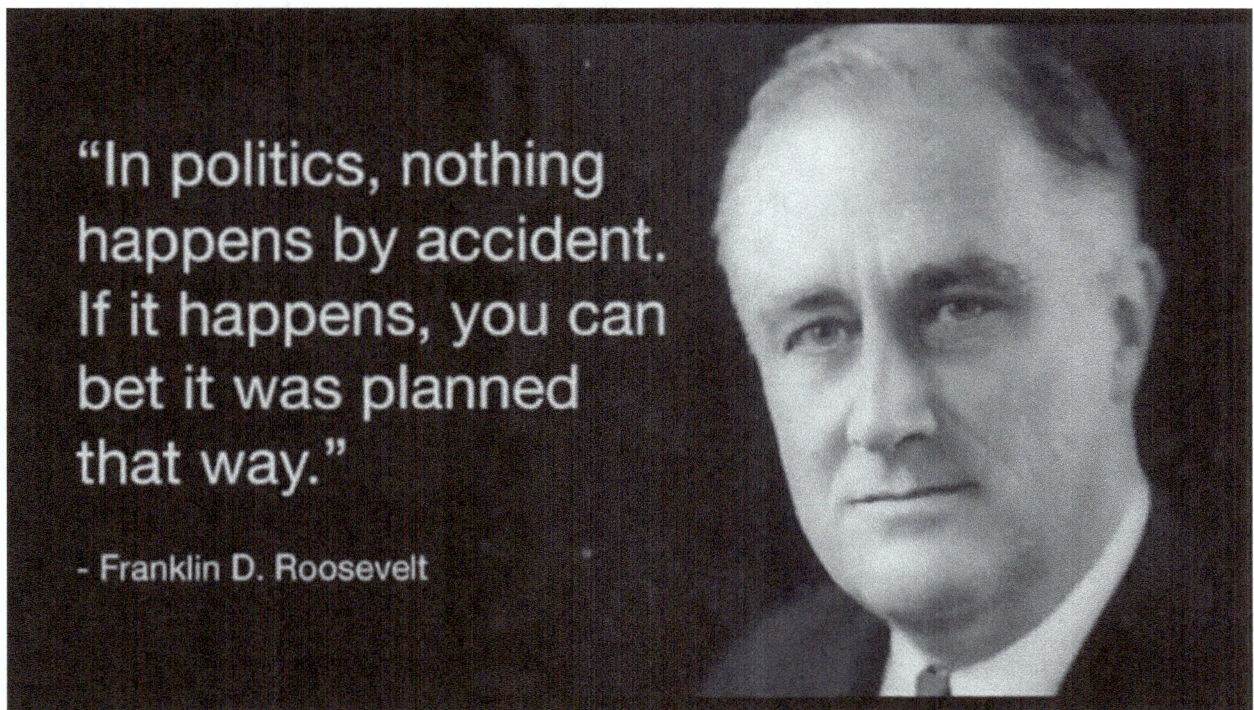

DOWNTURN OF US ECONOMY

- **UNEMPLOYMENT - 100 MILLION [JOBLESS ALLOWANCE]**

- **PEOPLE ON POVERTY LINE [FOOD STAMPS] - 95 MILLION**

- **MIDDLE CLASS ALMOST WIPED OUT / UNDER EMPLOYED (WORKING FOR LESS WAGES)**

- **CPI INDEX SHOWING COLLAPSE DUE TO TREMENDOUSLY LOW OIL PRICES**

- **MANUFACTURING ON DECLINE, GLOBAL TRADE ON DECLINE, ECONOMY IS ALREADY OUTSOURCED TO CHINA (PER PLAN!)**

- **BALTIC DRY INDEX SHARPLY ON DECLINE – NO SHIPS MOVEMENT TRANSATLANTIC**

- **BIG RETAILERS [WALLMARTS] CLOSING HUNDREDS OF STORES, FOLLOWED LONG LIST OF COMPANIES**

- **TRUCKING / LOGISTICS INDUSTRY ON SHARP DECLINE - 48% [LESS MOVEMENT], CORONA PLANDEMIC (ENGINEERED) WORSENED THE SITUATION!**

OTHER FINANCIAL IMPACTS

- **European Economies Are On The Downslide Like Spain, Italy, France, UK, While Greece And Cyprus Are Already Collapsed!**

<u>Recent, Ukraine – Russia War (off-course planned) has already crippled European Economy!</u>

- **Germany Is Deliberately Hit By The Migrant Crisis And Tremendous Budgeting For NATO and <u>Current Ukraine- Russia Conflict!</u>**

- **Bank Bail-Ins Have Been Started In Europe, Followed By US**

- **<u>Banks Preparing For Emergency Scenarios</u> – Bank Holiday, Economic Collapse, Credit / Debit Cards Not Responding At ATMs And Counters**

- **Stock Exchanges And Derivative Markets In New York, London, China, Japan And Others Crashing**

- **60% Of Ships Are Docked At Chinese Ports (Worldwide recession!)**

- **War Of Currencies – Russia, China Dumping US$ Backed Assets And US$, Clear Threat To Artificial US$ Hegemony**

- **The De-pegging Of US$ By The OPEC Countries (If.....) <u>From Petro-Dollar Will be The Final Nail In The Coffin!</u>**

GENERAL TIPS FOR ECONOMIC SURVIVAL DURING UPCOMING CATASTROPHES / TRIBULATIONS!

- **<u>Get out of all sorts of Debt,</u> even the smallest amount on Credit Cards, which <u>off-course is Riba (usury)</u>!**

- **Individuals must keep <u>hard cash with them not in banks</u>, as banks will default in payments and usage of Cash /Debit / Credit Cards. Upcoming Central Bank Digital Currency (CBDC) to be introduced in USA, Europe and China will be done to <u>enslave humanity!</u>**

- **<u>Convert the Cash into "gold" and "silver" coins / bars</u>, as it is "real money" and always preserve your purchasing power!**

- **If possible, <u>purchase farmland</u> (for living and cultivation) and <u>move-out from the main cities, and adopt security measures!</u>**

- **If possible, have some <u>livestock</u> like goat, sheep, cow etc.**

- **<u>Grow your own food</u>** (preferably organic, avoid GM / Supermarket Food) and establish **<u>off-grid lifestyle</u>** to **<u>be independent</u>** (to maximum extent) form the oppressive authorities and off-course preparedness!

FOOD PREPARATIONS!!

A CLEAR WARNING - LIVING IN ANY PART OF THE WORLD!

Stock **Food Supplies** (depending upon family size) for at **least Six Months for any short-term (riots, chaos etc.)** and **medium-term crisis** (Imminent War Like Situation having Global Impact)!!!

Recommended and Not Limited to:

- **JERRY CANS (For Water Reservoir) - 25 L**

- **WATER PURIFICATION TABLETS**

- **RICE - 10 KG BAG**

- **PULSES - MISC. + SOUPS + NOODLES + BANANA CHIPS**

- **DRY FRUITS + BISCUITS**

- **DRIED MILK + ENERGY DRINK (ORANGE) +**

- **OAT / BARLEY**

- **COOKING OIL**

- **ROASTED BEANS**

- **MEDICAL KIT + VITAMINS + MEDICINES (NEEDY + GENERAL)**

- **SURVIVAL KIT + WARM CLOTHING + BLANKETS**

ISLAMIC PERSPECTIVE - زمان الاخر العلم [The Study of End Times]

"he (Muhammad SAWS) **does not speak from his own desire.**

It is but not pure revelation revealed by Allah (SWT)

AL QURAN: SURAH AI NAJAM, VERSE 3

IMPORTANCE OF ISLAMIC ESCHATOLOGY

☐ In-depth analysis leading to **interpretation** of major and minor Signs before the Hour (Assa'a) / End of Time, using "**proper methodology**" (covering broad spectrum of knowledge from **Quran, Authentic Hadith / Tradition, International Monetary Economics, International Relations & Politics, Geo-politics, and History)** which include:

☐ **Minor Signs** mentioned in **Hadith / Tradition - e – Jibril / Arch Angel Gabriel**

☐ **10 Major Signs:** Dajjal, Coming of Hazrat Essa (A.S.), Gog and Magog, Beast coming from the land, Sun rising from the West, Dukhan (Smoke),

Three Major Earthquakes [one in the East, one in the West and one in Arabia] and Fire coming from Yemen that will drive the people to the place of Assembly

- **Major Benefits:**

    - Awareness of "**End Times**" and its distinction with "**End of History**

    - Understanding the "**Age of Fitan (current)**" by differentiating between "**Reality**" and "**Deception**", **interpreting "Religious Symbolism**" rather merely accepting "**Literally**", Signs / Prophecies mentioned in Hadith / Tradition

    - **Warning** from every kind of "**Fasad**" (destruction) in the End Times / Age of Fitan!

    - Possibility of safeguarding the most important asset of a believer (Momin) – **Emaan!**

    - **Islamic point of view without boxing gloves (Tafarqa / mutual differences) and open to positive criticism for enhancing / improving and promoting true knowledge (Haq)!**

ALMOST 100 SIGNS / PROPHECIES OF

OUR BELOVED PROPHET MUHAMMAD (peace be upon him and progeny) PERTAINING TO <u>AGE OF FITAN (END TIMES)</u> **HAVE BEEN FULFILLED!!!**

HENCE, WE ARE LIVING IN END TIMES!

<u>If The Current World State Of Affairs Are Considered To Be Happening By Accident Then..</u>

"Many are the Jinn and men we have made for Hell; They have hearts wherewith they understand not, eyes wherewith they see not, and ears wherewith they hear not. They are like cattle,- nay but they are worse!

HADEES E JIBRIL AS (AUTHENTIC TRADITION)

"On the authority of Umar who said: One day while we were sitting with the Messenger of Allah (peace be upon him and his progeny), there came before us a man with extremely white clothing and extremely black hair. There were no signs of travel on him and none of us knew him. He [came and] sat next to the Prophet (s). He supported his knees up against the knees of the Prophet (s) and put his hand on his thighs. He said, 'O Muhammad, tell me about Islam.'

The Messenger of Allah (peace be upon him and his progeny) said,

'Islam is to testify that there is none worthy of worship except Allah and that Muhammad is the Messenger of Allah (peace be upon him and his progeny), to establish the prayers, to pay the zakat, to fast [the month of] Ramadan, and to make pilgrimage to the House if you have the means to do so.' He said, 'You have spoken truthfully [or correctly].' We were amazed that he asks the question and then says that he had spoken truthfully. He said, 'Tell me about Emaan (faith).' He [the Messenger of Allah (peace be upon him and his progeny)] responded, 'It is to believe in Allah, His angles, His books, His messengers, the Last Day and to believe in the divine decree, [both] the good and the evil thereof.' He said, 'You have spoken truthfully.' He said, 'Tell me about al-Ihsaan (goodness).' He [the Prophet (peace be upon him and his progeny)] answered, 'It is that you worship Allah as if you see Him. And even though you do not see Him, [you know] He sees you.' <u>He said, 'Tell me about [the time of] the Hour,' He [the Prophet (peace be upon him and his progeny)] answered, 'The one being asked does not know more than the one asking.' He said, 'Tell me about it's signs.</u>' He answered, <u>'The slave-girl shall give birth to her mistress, and you will see the barefooted, scantily clothed, destitute shepherds competing in constructing lofty buildings.'</u> Then

he went away. I stayed for a long time. Then he [the Prophet (peace be upon him and his progeny)] said, 'O Umar, do you know who the questioner was?' I said, 'Allah and His Messenger know best.' He said, 'It was [the angel] Gabriel who came to teach you your religion.' (Sahih Muslim)

DAJJAL's (ANTICHRIST) RULE

Holy Prophet (peace be upon him and his progeny) said:

"The false Messiah / Antichrist (Dajjal) would **live on earth for 40 days** (i.e., after his release from his chains) in which **one day would be like a year, one day would be like a month, one day would be like a week, and all (the rest of) his days would be like your days.**" (Sahih Muslim)

<u>**Interpretation:**</u>

- ✓ 1 Day like a year   – Pax Britannica   - **(1095 CE - 1918 CE)**

- ✓ 1 Day like a month – Pax Americana   - **(1918   CE –   2001CE**)

- ✓ 1 Day like a week –   Pax Judaica   - **(2001 CE – 2023 CE)**

- ✓ Remaining (37 Days) like all our days – Pax Satanica (Dajjalian Rule or NEW WORLD ORDER)

DAJJAL'S (ANTICHRIST) MISSION!

Jews have always believed that their **promised Messiah** will come to do few things to bring back the promised "Golden age" by establishing the **Ruling State of the World in Jerusalem**. These are as follows:

- Liberating the land for the Jews

- Bringing the Jews back for settlement

- Construction of Temple in Bait Al Maqdas (Jerusalem)

- Placement of the Throne of Prophet Daud a.s.

- Restoring Israel (promised land) as the Ruling State of the World like Prophet Daud a.s.

Now, we have seen from our very own eyes or read in any authentic source of history that although **their Jewish Messiah** (according to them) has not yet arrived yet, therefore the **events destined to culminate toward the State of Israel becoming the Ruling State of the World are unfolding in this direction!** How is it possible? Is there any logical / authentic explanation for these events or they had been happening just by accident?

We have observed **these events unfolding sequentially** as follows:

- Creation of Zionist Movement in 1897 in Basel, Switzerland by the European Jews (not Bani Israelis, but Khazarian Jews!)

- The Jews conspired for **World War I** and achieved in:

  - Bringing **Jewish Financed Bolshevik Revolution** (Communism) in Russia – 1917 CE

- **Destroying the Ottoman Empire** to pave the way of Jews settlement in Palestine

- **Securing Balfour Declaration on November 2, 1917-** Letter from British Foreign Secretary Arthur James Balfour to Lord Rothschild (Chairman Zionist Movement) that made public the British support of a Jewish homeland in Palestine!

- **Capturing Jerusalem** through the British (General Allenby) - **December 1917**

- **Liberating the land for the Jews** (Europeans in majority) and bringing them for settlement (illegal) after **almost 2000 years**

- Creation of **Secular** Muslim Nation States through **Arab Nationalism (across Middle East)**

- Bringing down Britain from being the ruling state of the world with pound sterling as the major currency – **Pax Britannica,** thus paving the way to the **USA, as the next ruling state of the world!**

- The Balfour Declaration led the **League of Nations** to entrust the United Kingdom with the **Palestine Mandate in 1922**

- **World War II -** As a mopping-up vast military operation by the Zionists to bring an end to Britain's world rule and bring about a new ruling state of the world –USA (Pax Americana) with **US Dollar** as the major currency of the world. Not to forget that for these "evil Jewish bankers", "war is profiteering business till date"!

TRIALS AND WARNINGS ABOUT DAJJAL:

- "And fear the 'Fitnah / Trial' which **affects not in particular those of you who do wrong (but it may afflict all the good & bad people together)** and know that Allah is severe in punishment."
(Verse No. 25, Surah Al-Anfal, Chapter No. 8, Holy Qur'an).

☐ Narrated by Hazrat Aishah (RA): I heard Allah's Messenger (peace and

blessings of Allah be upon him and his progeny) in his Salat / Prayers, seeking refuge with Allah from the Fitnah of 'Ad-Dajjal'. (Hadith No. 7129, Book of Al-Fitan, Sahih Bukhari, Vol. 9)

☐ Between the creation of Adam (AS) and the onset of the Hour, there is no creation that has more impact than the 'Dajjal' – (Hadith No. 7395 , Book of Tribulations & Portents of the Hour, Sahih Muslim, Vol. 7)

☐ Narrated Anas (RA): The Prophet (peace and blessings of Allah be upon him and his progeny) said, **"No Prophet was sent but that he warned his followers against the one-eyed liar (i.e. 'Dajjal')........."** (Hadith No. 7131, Book of Al-Fitan, Sahih Bukhari, Vol. 9)

COMMENTS:

It can clearly be understood that all Prophets sent by Allah SWT (The Most High) have warned about the trials and tribulations of "Dajjal". This means that this subject is very serious, as this "creation" of Allah SWT is meant to test the entire mankind at its peak, especially in the **End times** and those who have faith and Noor (spiritual insight / light) will survive in End times (Akhir uz zaman) in shaa Allah! May Allah SWT make us among the faithful ones - Ameen ya Rab Al Aalameen!

Has Not The Time Yet Arrived That We Pay Attention To The Subject Of Islamic Eschatology (Study Of End Times), Specially Understanding The Worst Of All Fitan / Trial In The History Of Mankind - "Dajjal"?

So It Is Still Time To Wake up!!!

DESTRUCTION OF ARABS!!

Hazrat Zainab bint Jahsh (RA) reported that Allah's apostle (peace and blessings of Allah be upon him and his progeny), **got up**

from sleep with a flushed red face and said:

"Woe be to the Arabs for the great evil that is approaching (them); the barrier of <u>Gog and Magog has opened</u> so much'. And Sufyan (RA) made a sign of ten with the help of his hand (to indicate the width of the gap) and I said: 'Allah's Messenger, would we be perished in spite of the fact that there would be good people amongst us'? Thereupon he said: 'Of course, but only when the evil predominates'." - (Sahih Bukhari & Sahih Muslim)

FOLLOWERS OF GOG AND MAGOG WILL GO TO HELL FIRE!!!!

Hazrat Abu Saeed Khudri narrates that the Messenger of Allah (peace be upon him and his progeny) said, "On the Day of

Judgement, Allah SWT will tell Adam to pick out the Jahanamis (people of Hell) from his progeny. Adam will ask, "O Allah, who are they?" Allah SWT will say,"999 out of 1000 are hell fire, while the one is for paradise." On hearing this the Sahaba overtaken by fear asked, "Who will the ONE for paradise be?" The Prophet replied, "Do not grieve, the 999 will be from Yajuj Ma'juj (Gog and Magog), while you will be the one for paradise." - (Sahih Bukhari / Sahih Muslim)

Has Not The Time Yet Arrived That We Pay Attention To The Subject Of "Gog And Magog ?"

SO IT IS STILL TIME TO WAKEUP!!!!

DR. ALLAMA IQBAL's VISION / VIEWS (POETRY) ON AGE OF FITAN / YA'JOOG AND MA'JOOJ (GOG AND MAGOG)

In 1917, Allama Iqbal early warned the Muslims about coming chaos, turmoil, and destruction in the whole world. Iqbal was the first one

<u>**who immediately responded to the 'Balfour Declaration of 1917' passed by the British Parliament**</u> **in which, British Foreign Secretary Balfour requested Baron Rothschild, a leader of British Jewish community, for a <u>Jews homeland</u> in Palestine (Israel).**

محنت و سرمایہ دنیا میں صف آراء ہو گئے   دیکھیے ہوتا ہے کس کس کی تمناؤں کا خون

حکمت و تدبیر سے یہ فتنہ بے آشوب خیز   ٹل نہیں سکتا، وقد کنتم یہ تستعجلون

أَثُمَّ إِذَا مَا وَقَعَ أَمَنْتُم بِهِ آلْآنَ وَقَدْ كُنْتُم بِهِ تَسْتَعْجِلُونَ ۝

کیا پھر جب عذاب واقع ہو چکے گا تب اس پر یقین کرو گے اب قائل ہوئے اور تم اسی کا تقاضا کرتے تھے ف۶

Verse of Quran: Surah Younus, Verse 51

کھل گئے یاجوج اور ماجوج کے لشکر تمام   چشمِ مسلم دیکھ لے تفسیرِ حرفِ ینسلون

The genius of Allam Iqbal <u>was able to correlate this</u> "strange event" in <u>the British Parliament with the following Quranic Verses</u> (interpretation), which no Muslim Scholar in the world could comprehend and do so!!!

إِذَا حَتَّىٰ (يَرْجِعُونَ لَا أَنَّهُمْ أَهْلَكْنَاهَا قَرْيَةٍ عَلَىٰ وَحَرَامٌ يَنسِلُونَ حَدَبٍ كُلِّ مِّن وَهُم وَمَأْجُوجُ يَأْجُوجُ فُتِحَتْ)

It has been ordained against **a town** that **We have destroyed**

that they shall not return (to enjoy a new lease of life)

until **Gog and Magog are let loose**, and begin swooping from

every mound

Al Quran: Surah 21: Verse 95

EUPHRATES THE BATTLE GROUND OF GREAT WARS!!!

Abu Hurayrah said,

**"The Prophet Muhammad (peace be upon him and his progeny) said,
'The Hour will not come before the Euphrates uncovers a mountain of
gold, for which people will fight. 99 out of 100 will die, but everyone
among them will say that perhaps he will be the one who will survive."**

- (Sahih Muslim)

Narrated Ubayy ibn Ka'b:

**I heard Allah's Final Prophet (peace be upon him and his progeny)
said: The Euphrates would soon uncover a mountain of gold and
when the people would hear of it, they would flock towards it but the
people who would possess that (treasure) (would say): If we allow
these persons to take out of it they would take away the whole of it.
So they would fight and ninety-nine out of one hundred would be
killed.**

(Muslim Book No: 40 No: 6922)

❖ <u>**TREMENDOUS OIL RESRVES**</u> **HAVE BEEN DISCOVERED IN GOLAN HEIGHTS – SYRIAN – ISRAELI BORDERING AREAS**

❖ <u>**30 TRILLION CUBIC FEET OF GAS RESERVES**</u> **HAVE BEEN ESTIMATED / DISCOVERED IN EGYPT (MEDITERRANEAN SEA)**

THE COUNT DOWN OF MALHAMA / ARMAGEDON / WWIII

And there is <u>no city but that We will destroy</u> it <u>before the Day of Resurrection or punish it with a severe punishment.</u> That has ever been in the <u>Register inscribed</u>."   - (Sura Al Isr'a: Verse: 58)

A <u>war of mass destruction </u>(WMDs / Nuclear / Thermo- Nuclear) is also indicated by the following verse from Holy Quran and sayings of the Holy Prophet (PBUH) that is 'Smoke' <u>being one of the Signs of the end of times:</u>

<u>"Then watch for the Day when the sky will bring a visible smoke. Covering the people; this is a painful torment.</u> (Holy Quran 44: 10,11)

Narrated by Hazrat Huzaifah (RA) that the Holy Prophet (PBUH) stated that:

"Qayamat (Day of Judgment) <u>will not come till you see ten signs</u>, which are: <u>Smoke which spreads throughout the East and West for forty days….</u>" - (Sahih Muslim)

TABLES WILL BE TURNED, IN SHAA ALLAH!

It was narrated that Ibn 'Umar (may Allah be pleased with him) said: "I heard the Messenger of Allah (peace be upon him and his progeny) say, 'The Jews will fight you and you will prevail over them, then a rock will say, "O Muslim! here is a Jew behind me, (come and) kill him." - Narrated by Al-Bukhari, no. 3593

Abu Huraira reported Allah's Messenger (may peace be upon him and his progeny) as saying: The last hour would not come unless the Muslims will fight against the Jews and the Muslims would kill them until the Jews would hide themselves behind a stone or a tree and a stone or a tree would say: Muslim, or the servant of Allah, there is a Jew behind me; come and kill him; but the tree Gharqad would not say, for it is the tree of the Jews- Sahih Muslim Book 041, Number 6985

CONQUEST OF CONSTANTINOPLE

Narrated Mu'adh ibn Jabal: The Prophet (peace be upon him and his progeny) said:

"The <u>flourishing state of Jerusalem will be when Yathrib (i.e., the city of Madinah) will be desolate; the desolate state of Yathrib will be when the great war comes; the outbreak of the great war will be (followed by) the conquest of Constantinople</u>; and the conquest of Constantinople will be (followed by) Dajjal's (Antichrist) coming forth (i.e., appearing, or emerging). He (the Prophet) then he tapped with his hand the thigh or the shoulder of the one to whom he was talking and said: This is certainly true like you are (sitting) here (he meant Mu'aadh ibn Jabal)"

- Sunan of Abu Dawud Book 37, Number 4281

MUSLIM RULERS / COUNTRIES MAKING FRIENDSHIP AND ALLIANCE WITH THE ZIONISTS!

"O you who have believed, <u>do not take the Jews and the Christians as allies</u>, when they become allies of one another. And whoever is an ally to them among you - then indeed, he is [one] of them. Indeed, Allah guides not the wrongdoing people." – Al Quran: Surah Al Ma'idah:51

<u>ALL THOSE NATIONS / LEADERS / GROUPS RECOGNIZE THE ILLEGITIMATE STATE OF ISRAEL ARE COMITTING BLASPHEMY (SHIRK), AS IT IS THE OUTCOME OF JUDEO- CHRSITIAN ZIONIST ALLIANCE, WARNED BY QURAN 1400 YEARS AGO!!!!</u>

CONCLUSION

☐ **Beware of mainstream media propaganda** – differentiate between appearance & reality (they are opposite in this Age of Fitan / End Times). **Alternative media is a better option**

☐ **Hold on to Quran and Authentic Sunnah** not only verbally but practically for preserving Emaan. **"O you who have attained to faith! Surrender yourselves wholly unto God, and follow not Satan's footsteps, for, verily, he is your open foe"** – Al Baqarah:208

☐ **Beware & protect yourselves / families /friends / community from the greatest fitnah in terms of Secularist Politics (western democracy), Interest Based Banking / Capitalist System, and Modern Western Global Civilization (feminist revolution / one-styled global society) - master minded by Dajjal and executed by his foot soldiers i.e.   Gog and Magog**

☐ **Istiqamat (stead fasting) is the key to survival in the ongoing and forthcoming severe trials and tribulations!!!**

- , which is being used to <u>destroy the Muslims within Muslim countries especially and other nations generally, by the Zionists to achieve their ultimate objectives</u> – United We Stand!

- it's high time to <u>pay attention and understand</u> the worldwide challenges through the <u>Study of Islamic Eschatology</u> (based on Quran & Authentic Sunnah), which <u>not only warns but provide authentic solution to the humanity!</u> – Ignorance is no Excuse!

Thank you for your kind attention, patience, and support!

With best regards,

Jazak Allah khairan kaseeran

For your kind feedback

ahsenala@gmail.com